This Book Belongs To

Terrabella Smoot and the unsung monsters

by Jon "Bean" Hastings

100% Pure

SMOOT'S

ICK

a fine blend of
GOO, SLOP, GRUNGE,
SLIME, MUCK, GRIME,
SLUDGE, GUNK & OOZE

S

Chapter One: Lost!

Terrabella Smoot's family was well known for their ick. They made ick that was so awfully icky that it had been called the finest ick in all the land. It was such good ick that Terrabella, her parents and even Grandpa Smoot had been invited to bring some of it to the Monster of the Year celebration in honor of Lord Thonk the Ghastly.

The Smoots had excitedly packed their best clothes, loaded the ick-making wagon and set off through Fangly Forest, headed for Ghastly Castle. Terrabella was so excited she could hardly sit still. She climbed onto the roof of the wagon, where she often liked to ride, and passed the time by thinking up new rhymes to describe her family's famous ick.

"Quick, pick Smoot's thick and slick ick for your next picnic!" said Terrabella.

"For ick with stick, Smoot's does the trick!" she sang.

"OOF!" she exclaimed a moment later.

Now "OOF!" is not something you would normally say to get folks to try your well-made ick. It is, however, the perfect thing to say if you've just been caught off guard, thumped soundly in the stomach and swept off an ick wagon by a tree branch.

"Hey, wait!" Terrabella yelled, clinging desperately to the branch.

But the wagon didn't wait and her family didn't hear her cries because the ick-maker was chugging away noisily.

Terrabella found herself stuck high in a tree with only catchy slogans about ick to keep her company.

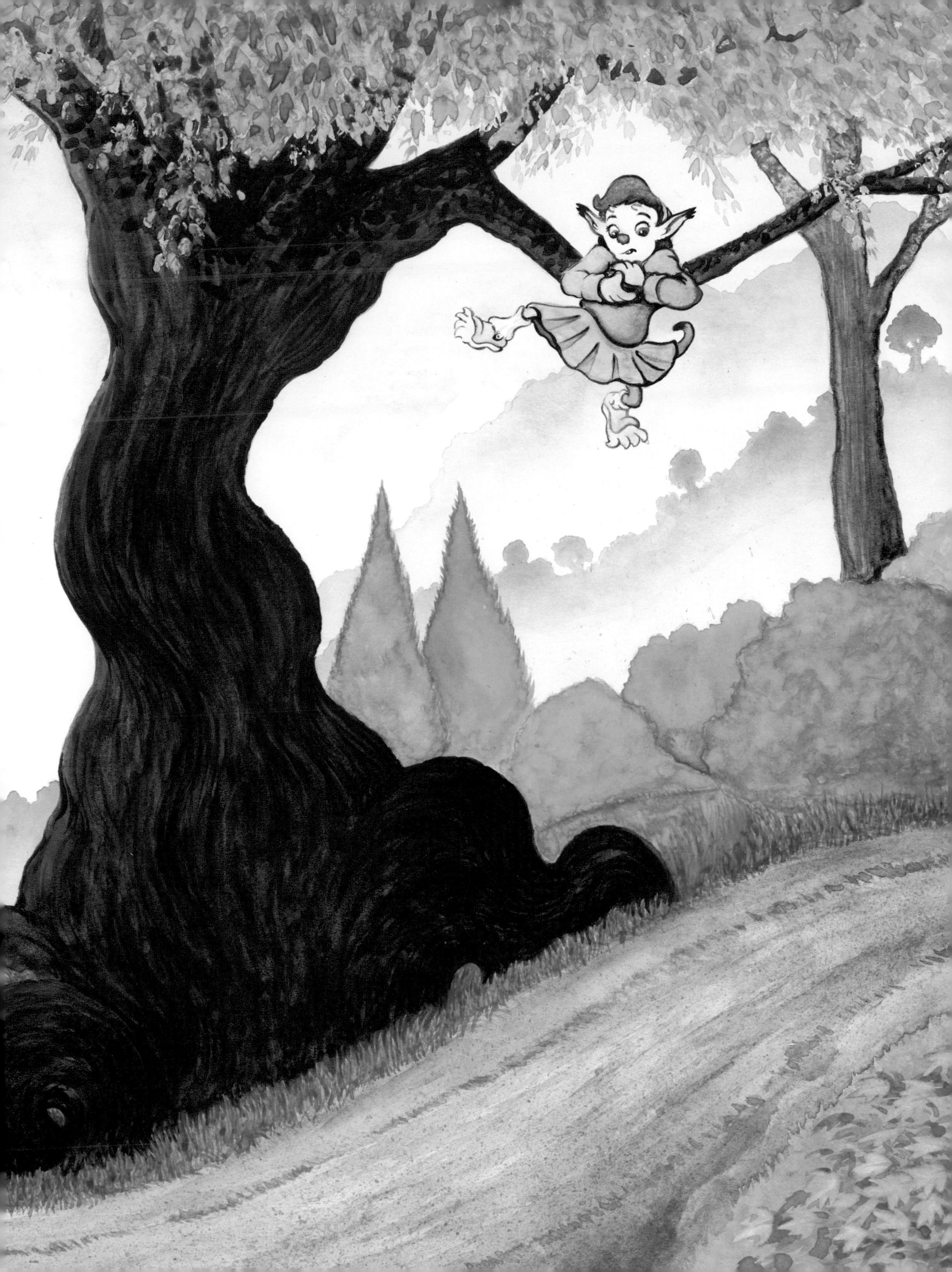

Looking down at the ground, Terrabella saw that it was quite a long way away. She realized that she might hurt herself if she tried to jump down. Being alone in the woods was one thing, but being alone in the woods and hurt was another thing entirely. Who knew what nasty beasties might be nearby?

Terrabella was worrying about what nasty beasties might be nearby when she heard something rustling in the bushes by the side of the road.

"Wh-who's there?" she asked the thing in the bushes.

"Spinach!" it replied.

"Spinach?" asked Terrabella, tightening her grip on the branch.

"Fiddle! Pudding! Boing!" it replied.

Terrabella was very confused by what the thing in the bushes was saying, and she was even more confused when it stumbled on to the road. The thing turned out to be a Flark bird and, as everyone knows, Flark birds can't talk.

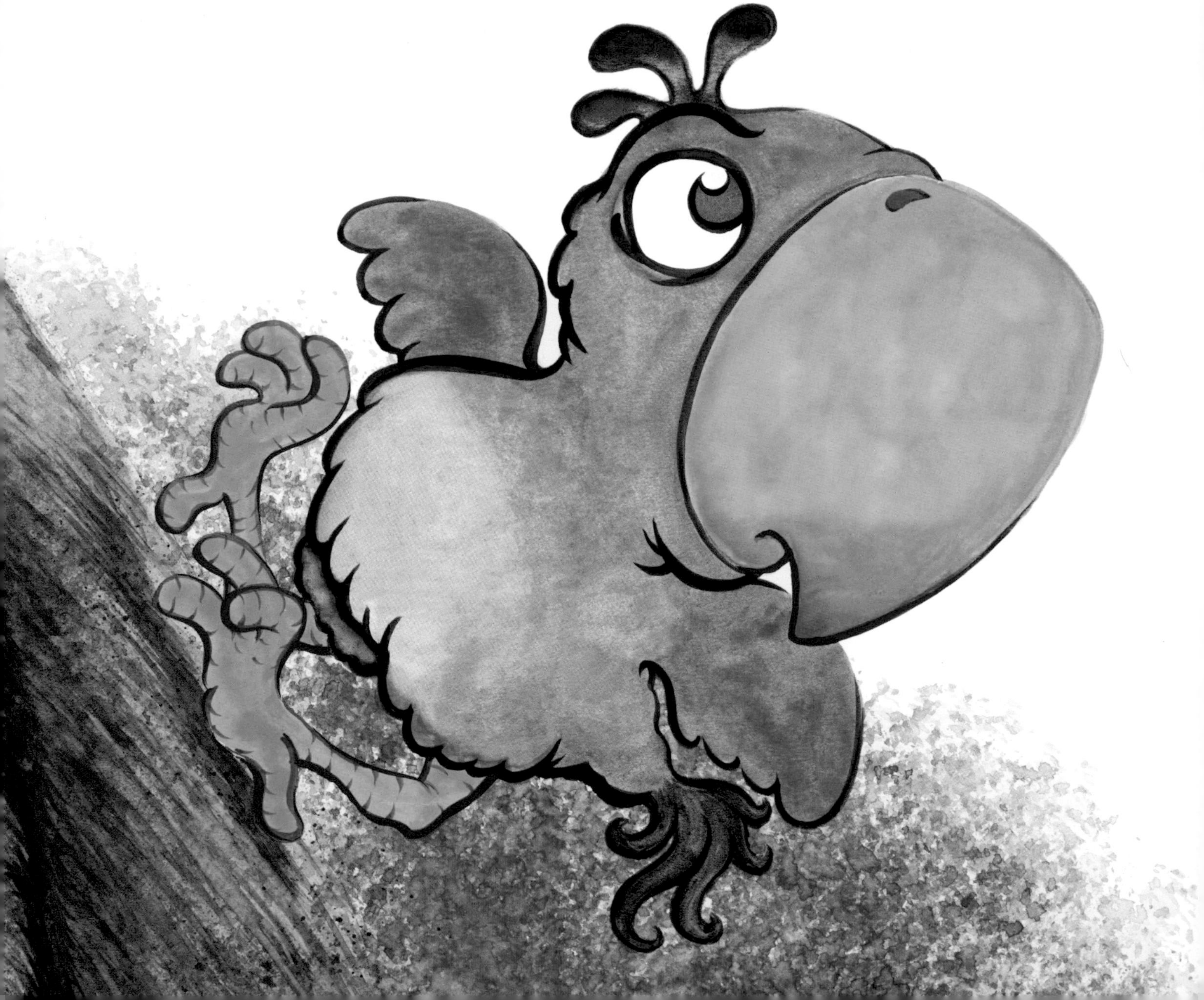

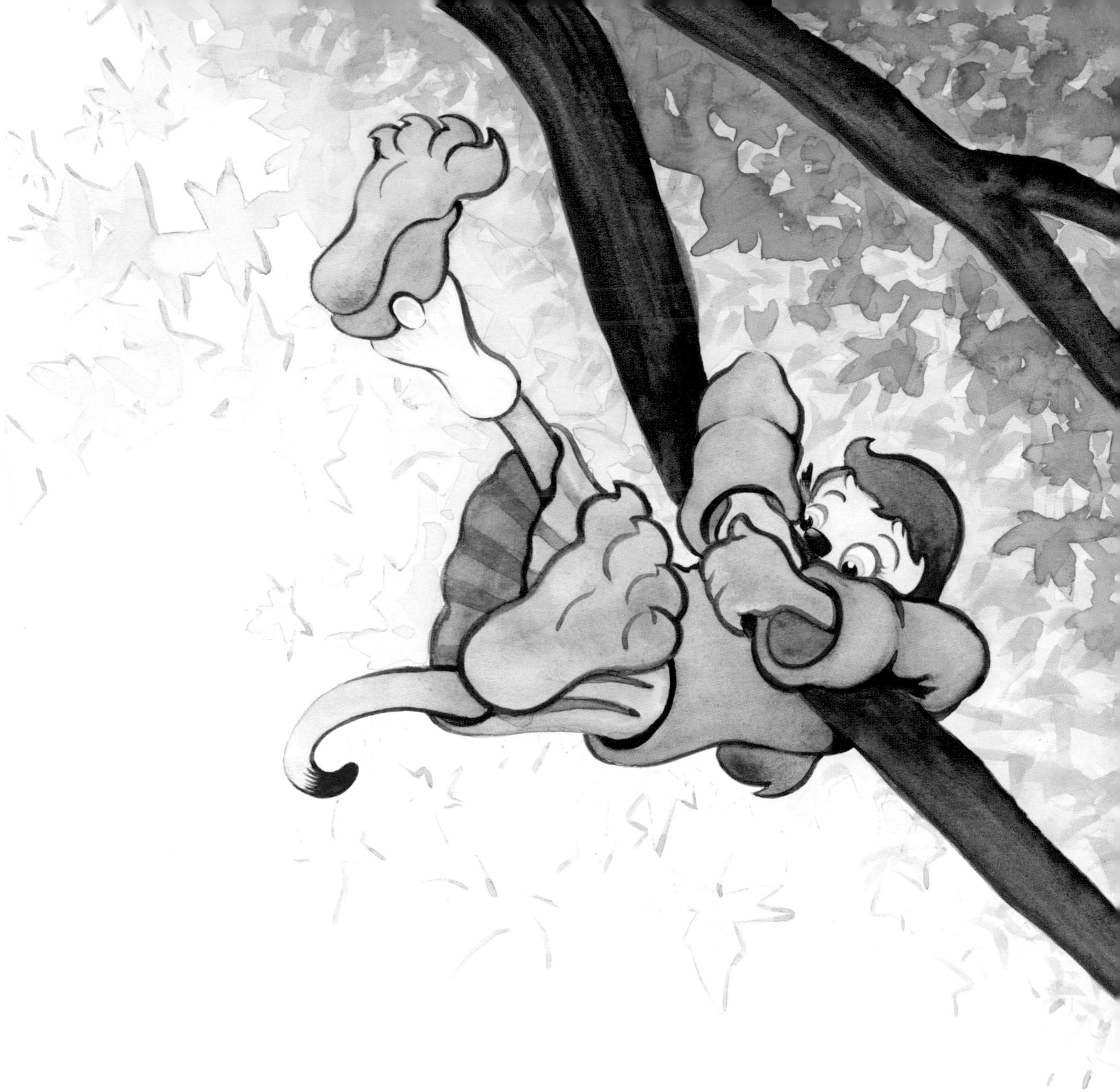

"Double stack of flapjacks!" said the Flark bird.

"Um, could you help me?" said Terrabella, a little unsure of what was going on. "I'm stuck in this tree and my family left without me and I'm losing my grip and..."

"Pie!" replied the Flark bird.

"Um, I'm sure I can get you some pie if you'd help me get down from here," said Terrabella.

"Zip! Zoom! Bing bang boom!" said the Flark bird as it stumbled underneath Terrabella.

"So, you're going to catch me then?" asked Terrabella doubtfully. Having little choice, she hung down as low as she could, closed her eyes tightly and let go of the branch.

Terrabella landed squarely on the Flark bird. She was unhurt by the feathery landing, but the Flark bird let out a pained

SQUAWK!!

along with a small, odd-looking monster. .

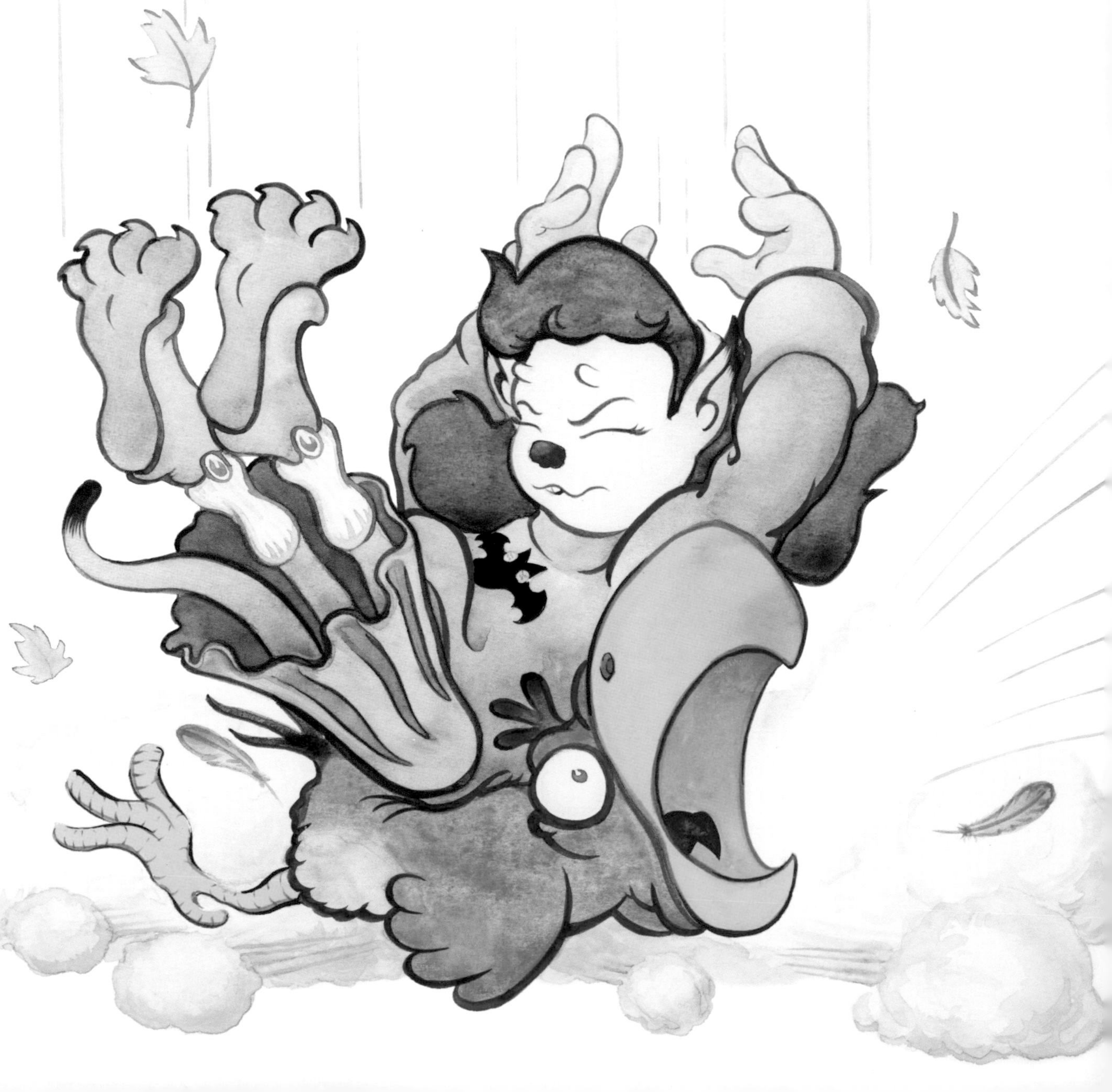

"Is it — whirligig! — morning already?" asked the small, odd-looking monster after it had bounced to a stop on the ground.

"Squaaaaaawk!" squawked the Flark bird angrily. Free of its passenger, it quickly flew away.

"What a rude Flark bird! — tweezers! — Not right in the head if you ask me. Completely bonkers, I'd say — oodles of noodles!" said the small, odd-looking monster.

Terrabella was not quite sure what to say. After a bit of thought, she decided that it would be best to simply introduce herself and ask the obvious question.

"Hello, I'm Terrabella Smoot," she said. "Is there something wrong with your brain?"

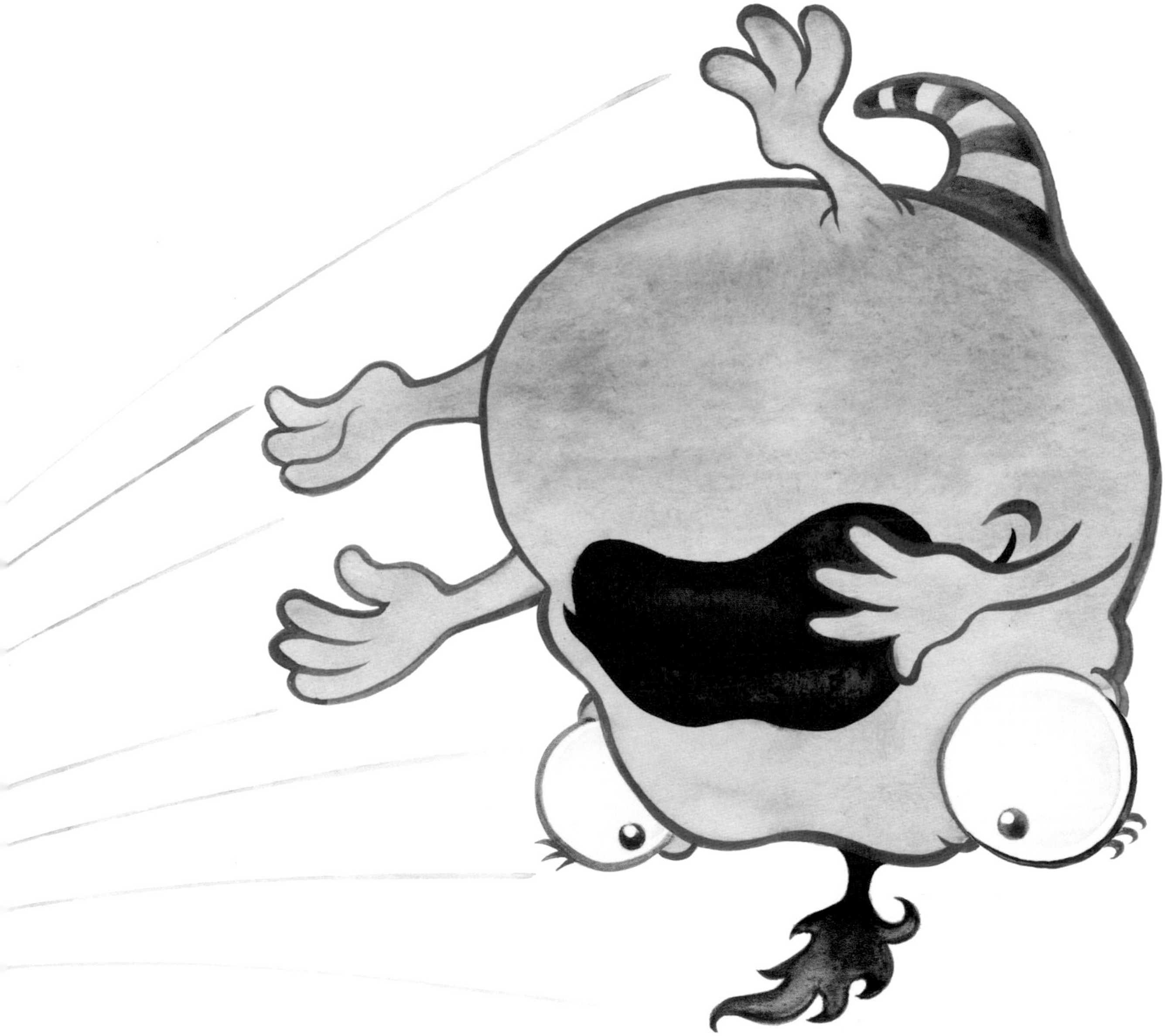

"My brain is perfectly fine — sponge! Humming along quite happily, thank you — goat! Allow me to introduce myself. I'm Eppie-Gladys Snarf — rutabaga!" said the small, odd-looking monster.

"I'm pleased to meet you, Eppie-Gladys Snarf Rutabaga," replied Terrabella, trying not to laugh at the small, odd-looking monster's odd-sounding name.

"No, no, no! — sizzle! Not 'Eppie-Gladys Snarf Rutabaga.' Just 'Eppie-Gladys Snarf,'" said Eppie-Gladys Snarf. "'Rutabaga' is just a word — fling!— I enjoy saying. Like 'sprocket' or 'goop.'"

"I see," said Terrabella, not really seeing at all.

"Well, it might need a bit of explaining — squid! — but we'd best get out of these woods," Eppie said. "Who knows what nasty beasties are nearby?"

"My family!" said Terrabella, remembering that she was lost in the woods.

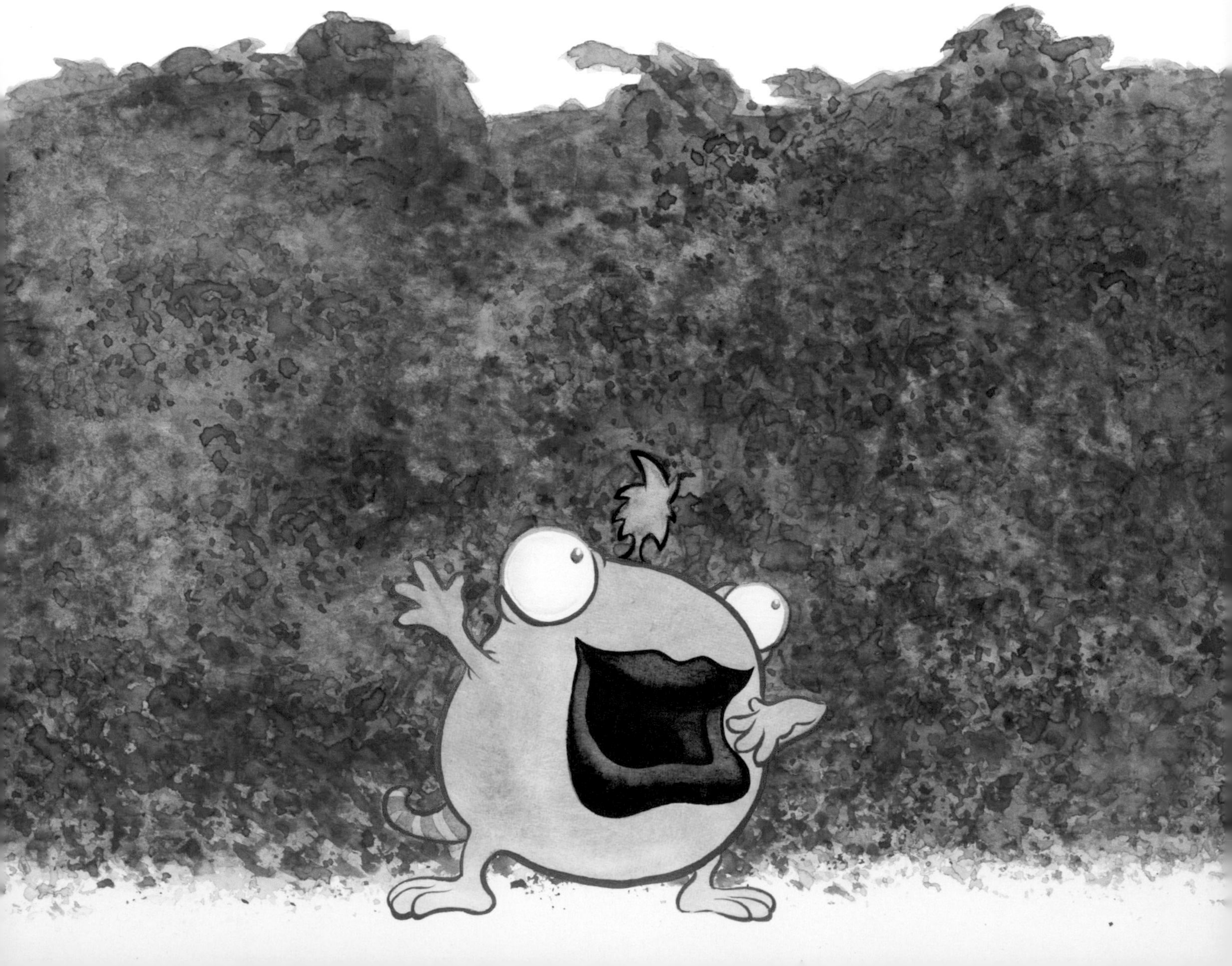

"You're family — zing! — are nasty beasties?" asked Eppie. "And they're — gulp! — nearby?" she said, looking around nervously.

"No, no!" said Terrabella, "My family are not nasty beasties that are nearby. . . . I mean, they aren't nasty beasties at all, and they are not nearby. They kept going without me."

"Well then, we'd best get a wiggle on — wiggle! — and catch up to them before it gets dark," said Eppie. "On the way, I'll tell you the gripping tale of myself."

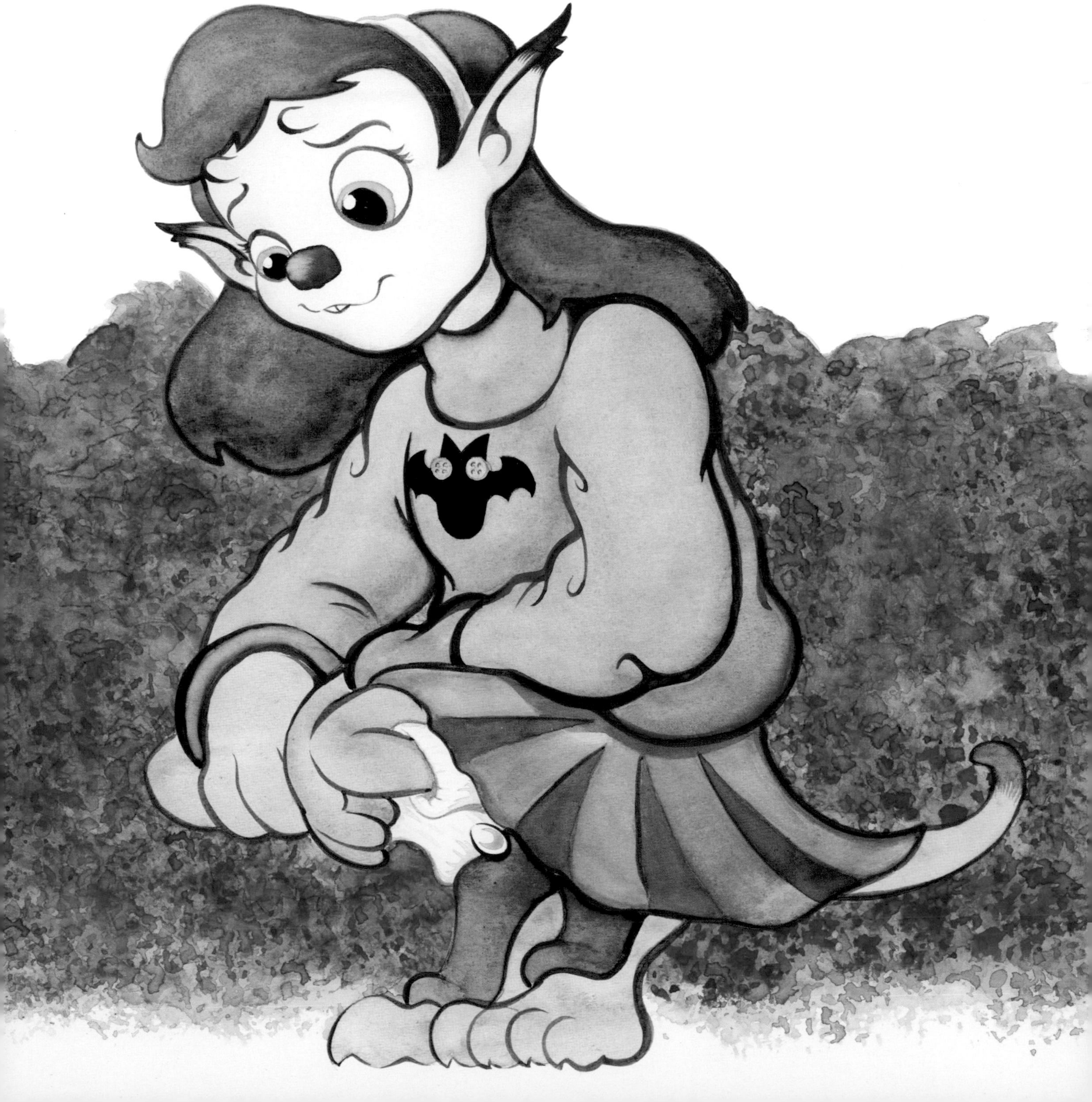

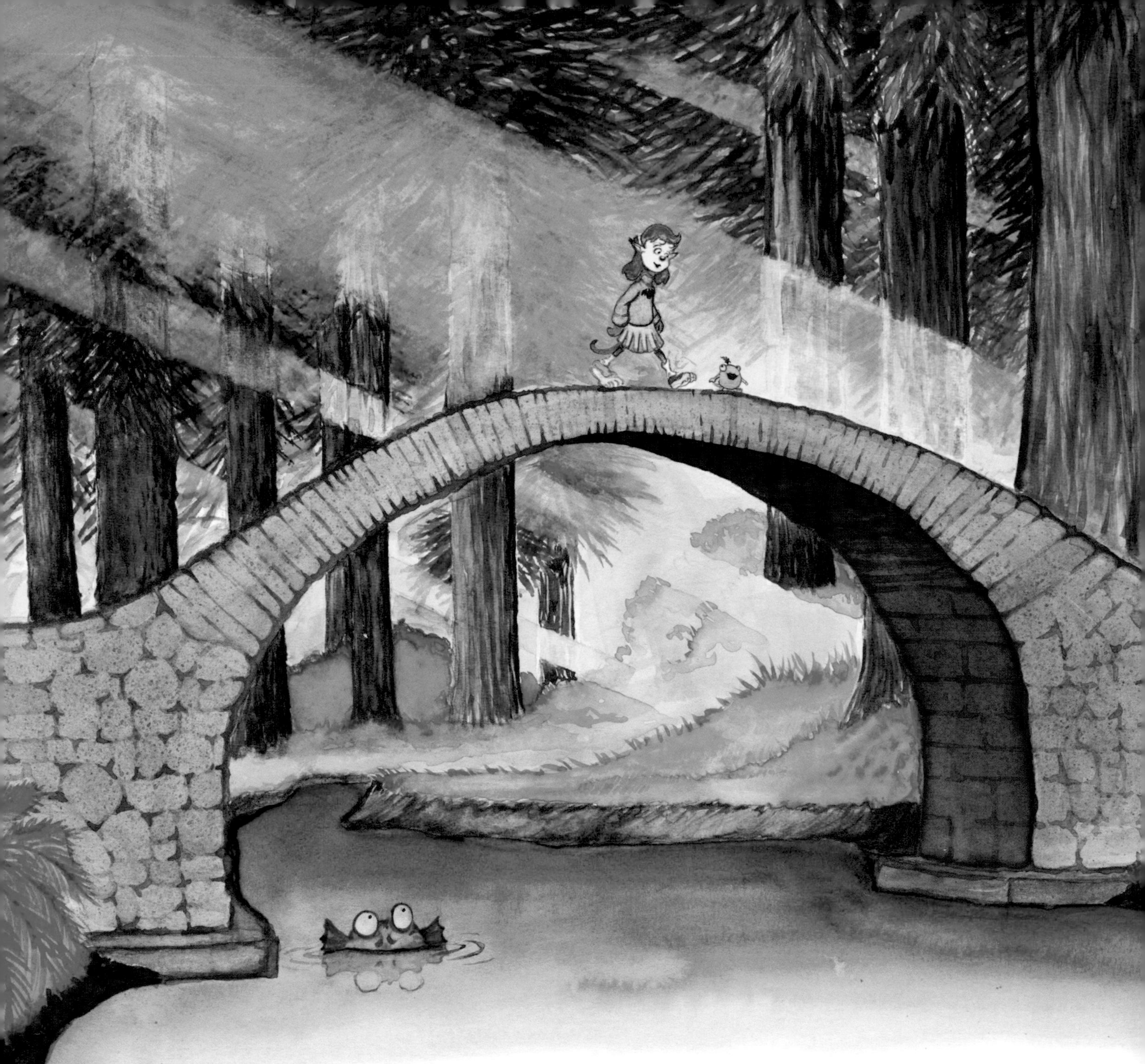

The two set out the way Terrabella's family had gone. Eppie had to run as fast as her little legs would carry her just to keep up. She didn't mind much, though, since she was pleased as ick punch to have someone to talk to.

"I come from a long line of Tight-Lipped Dipps," Eppie explained. "They have all been servants to —crinkle! — the lords of Ghastly Castle."

Terrabella stopped in her tracks and stared at Eppie in disbelief. "You work for Lord Thonk the Ghastly?" she said. "That must be so wonderful! He's so amazingly ghastly and brave! Eeeeee!"

"Well, yes," said Eppie, over Terrabella's excited squealing. "Anyway, I try to do my work but I tend to talk too much — squish! — and that gets me into trouble."

Terrabella started walking again. "But you said you are a Tight-Lipped Dipp," she said, "I thought Tight-Lipped Dipps barely ever spoke."

"Actually," replied Eppie, "I said that — cupcake! — I came from a long line of Tight-Lipped Dipps. You see I'm the very first Loose-Lipped Dipp and — fungus! — I just can't seem to keep my mouth shut. I like to yell words out

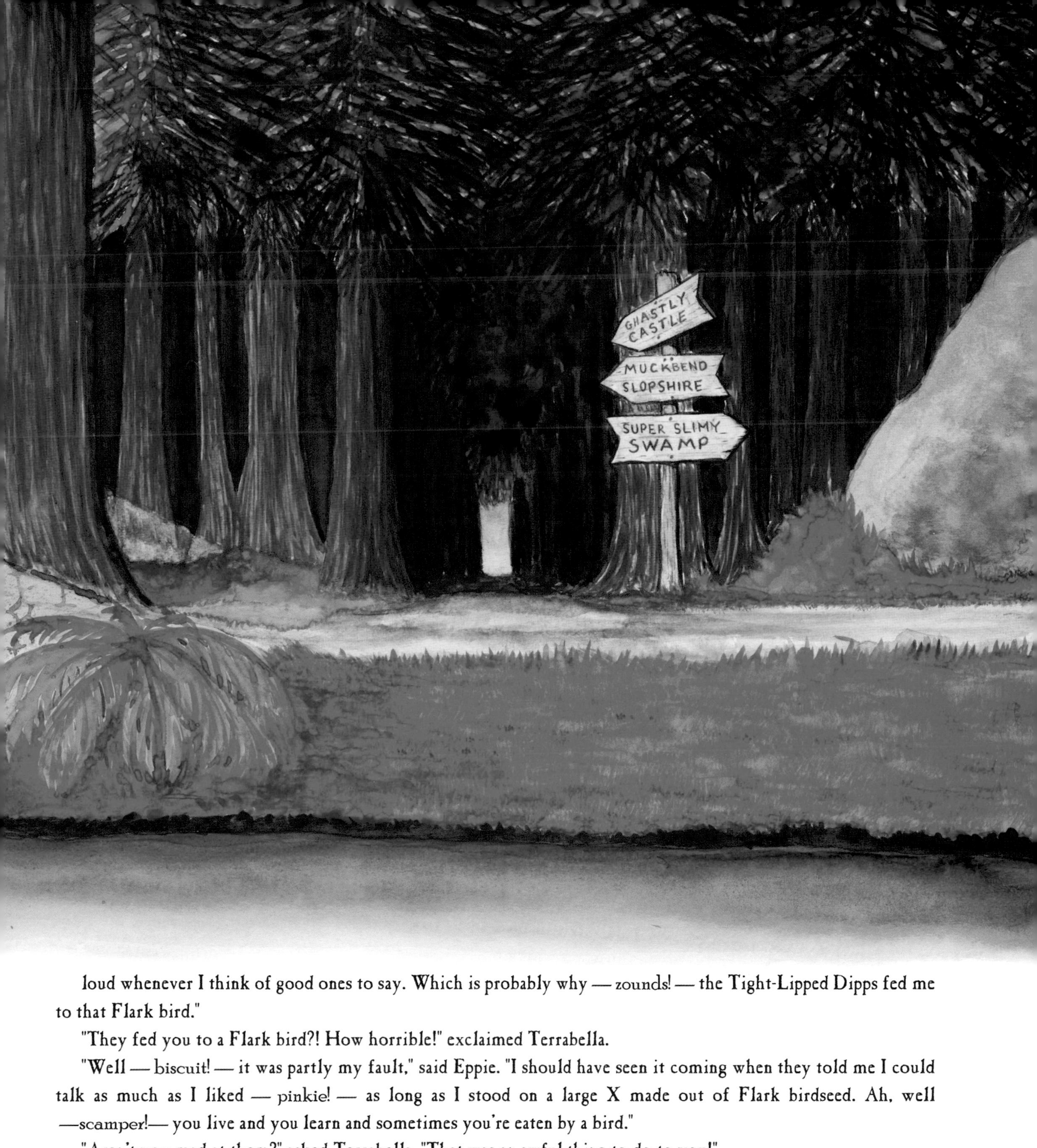
GHASTLY CASTLE
MUCKBEND
SLOPSHIRE
SUPER SLIMY SWAMP

loud whenever I think of good ones to say. Which is probably why — zounds! — the Tight-Lipped Dipps fed me to that Flark bird."

"They fed you to a Flark bird?! How horrible!" exclaimed Terrabella.

"Well — biscuit! — it was partly my fault," said Eppie. "I should have seen it coming when they told me I could talk as much as I liked — pinkie! — as long as I stood on a large X made out of Flark birdseed. Ah, well —scamper!— you live and you learn and sometimes you're eaten by a bird."

"Aren't you mad at them?" asked Terrabella. "That was an awful thing to do to you!"

"Actually — beep! — it was very nice in there," said Eppie. "It was warm and quite cozy really — doohickey! — and I could talk all I wanted. I just might — squelch! — retire to inside a Flark bird one day."

Although she was glad for the company, Terrabella was baffled by her strange new friend. But her bafflement would have to wait until later because they were coming to the edge of the woods.

"C'mon!" she said, breaking into a run.

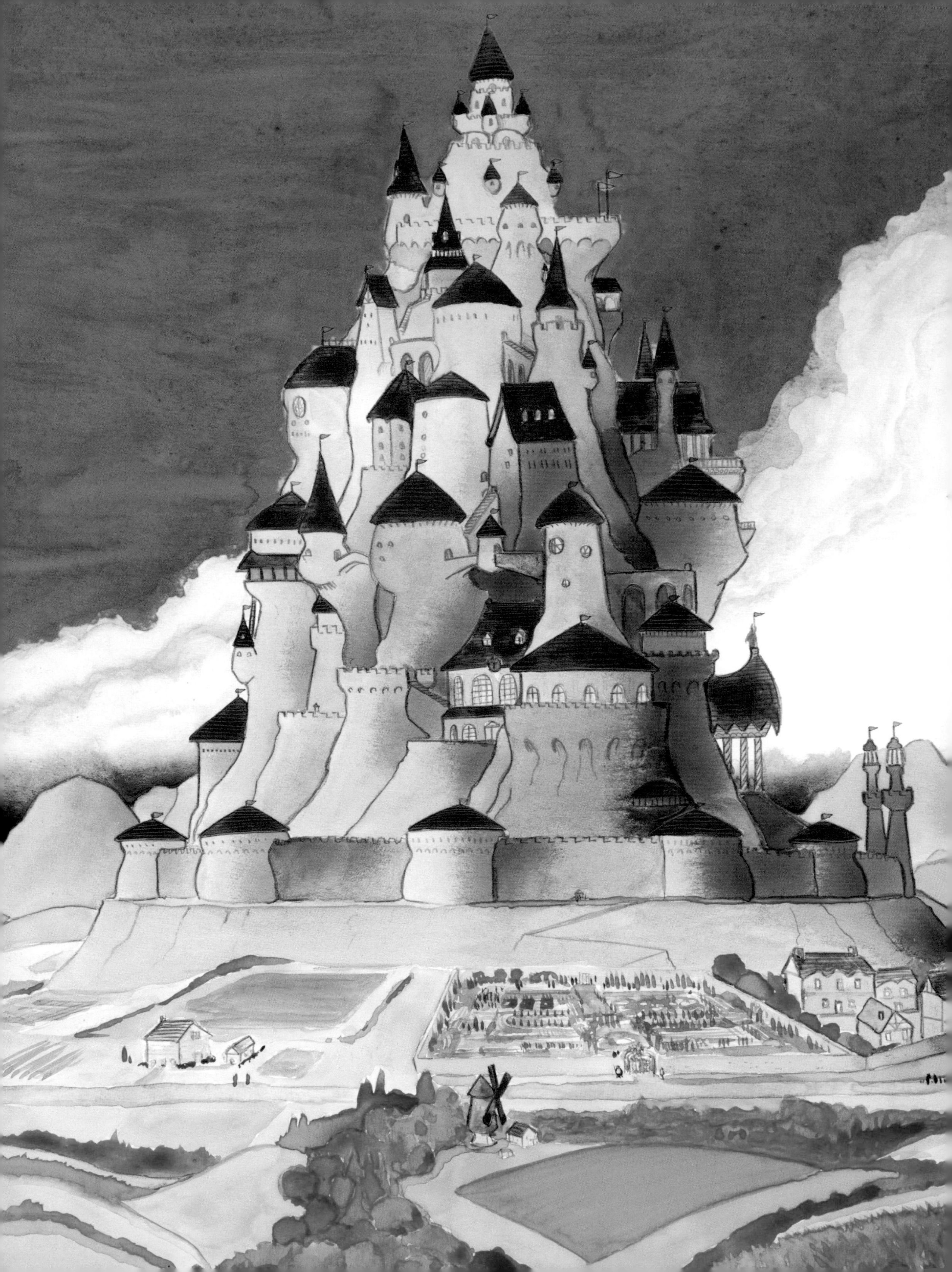

Chapter Two: Ghastly Castle

Terrabella was stunned by what she saw when they came out of the forest. There, looming menacingly in front of them, was Ghastly Castle. Coming from the small town of Muckbend, Terrabella had never seen a building taller than a mid-sized giant. Yet here was this monstrous lump of a fortress as big as a mountain. The castle's gray hugeness made the town of Ghastliville, which spread out in its shadow, seem as if it were cringing in fear. Terrabella shivered with the heebie-jeebies.

"Is — warthog! — that your family's wagon?" Eppie asked, excitedly pointing down the road.

"Yes! Yes, it is!" The thought of catching up to her family chased away Terrabella's fear of Ghastly Castle.

"It doesn't look like we'll reach them before they get to the city," said Eppie doubtfully.

Terrabella followed the road with her eyes and saw that Eppie was right. Her heart sank. In the city, with thousands of monsters gathered for the celebration that night, finding her parents would be very difficult indeed.

"We can — cheese! — go through the castle gardens," suggested Eppie, "I know — purple! — a shortcut."

Terrabella wasn't sure it was the best idea, but it seemed to be the only way to catch up. "All right," she said bravely. "Let's go."

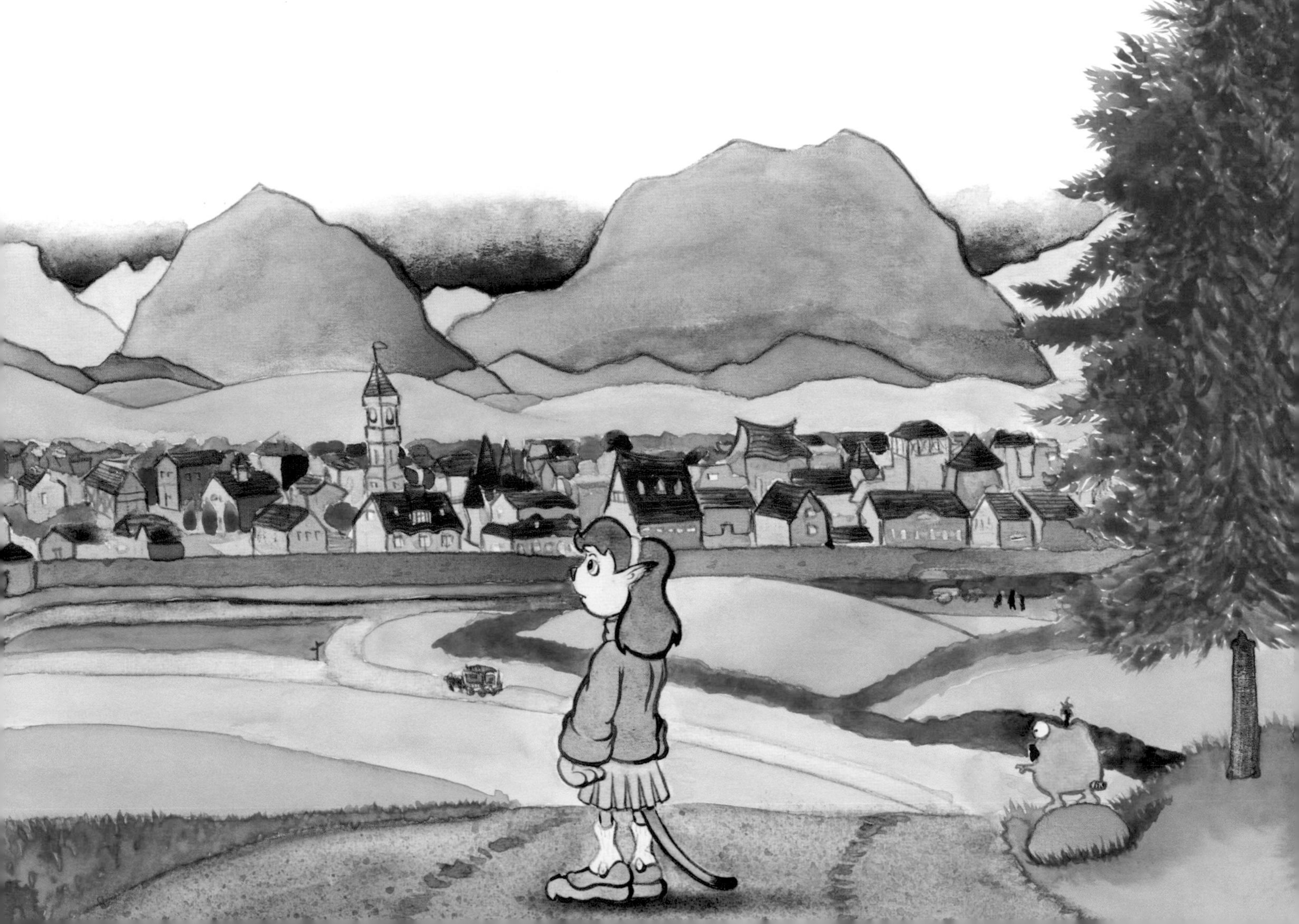

Terrabella and Eppie hid behind a bush across from the huge garden gates where two large guards stood holding sharp and pointy spears.

"How are we going to get in?" whispered Terrabella.

"We'll just have to — gobbledygook! — quietly sneak in," replied Eppie. Unfortunately, she had yelled out the word "gobbledygook" in the middle of her sentence. This had alerted the guards that someone was up to something and whatever that something was, they were up to it in the bush right in front of them.

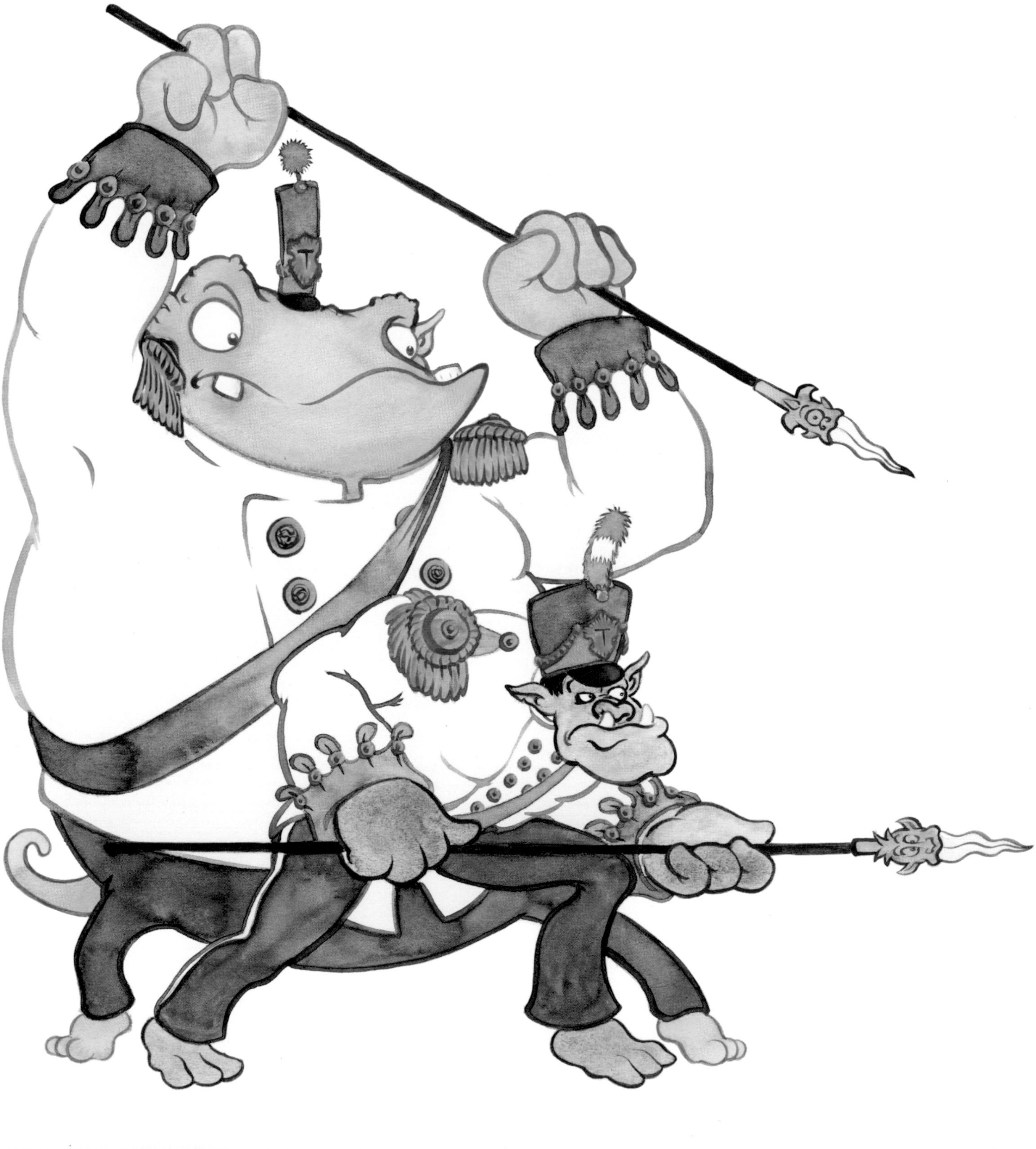

The guards lowered their sharp and pointy spears, and the uglier of the two shouted towards the bush, "When's there?!"

"I think you mean '*Who's* there?'" said the other guard, who was quite ugly, but not as ugly as the first.

"Hmmm, me thinks you're right," said the first, uglier guard. "Me never remember how that go."

Behind the bush, Terrabella had turned quite pale and Eppie could do nothing but run around in a small circle, whispering loudly, "What do we do?! What do we do?! What do we do?! — hullabaloo! — What do we do?!"

"Are you an enchanted talking bush," asked the less-ugly guard, "or something in the bush that's just chatty?"

"Either way, we poke you a lot now!" said the really ugly guard. The guards lumbered towards the bush with their sharp and pointy spears perfectly poised for poking.

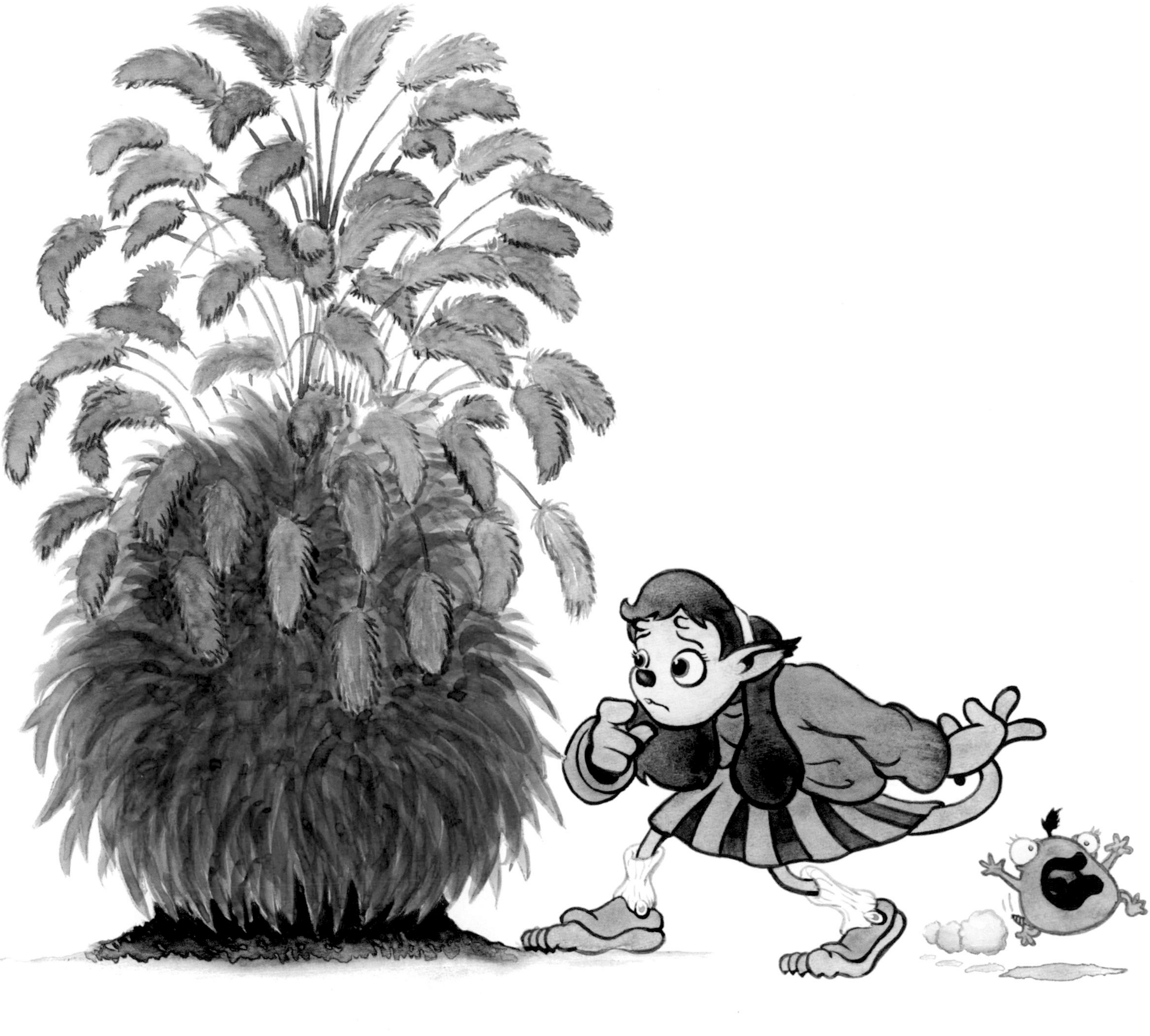

Having heard the guards speak, Terrabella knew they were not exactly super-geniuses. This gave her an idea.

Terrabella quickly scooped Eppie up and placed her on top of her head. She then took her sweatshirt and pulled it up to Eppie's waist. "Hold on to my collar and move your lips when I talk," whispered Terrabella, and she boldly stepped out from behind the bush, right square in front of the guards.

"Yes, well, that bush meets all royal bushy standards and requirements," said Terrabella through the front of her sweatshirt as Eppie moved her lips. "Ah, good! Glad to see you guards are paying attention. Now then, I'll just pop into the royal garden there and check the giant stinkweeds for royal stinkiness then."

"Wait!" said the uglier guard. "Where are you?!"

"Why, I'm right here!" replied Terrabella.

"I think he means, "*Who* are you?!" said the less ugly yet still quite ugly guard.

"Yeah, what he says," said the more ugly guard, waving his spear in little, pointy circles at Terrabella and Eppie.

"I am, of course, um . . . Eppibella Smoolip!" said Terrabella. "I am the royal plant inspector for his most Frightful Terribleness, Lord Thonk the Ghastly! Now, if you'll excuse me, there's some stinkweed in that garden that needs inspecting, and it needs inspecting now! We can't have less than perfect stink for the Monster of the Year, now can we?"

With that, she marched off toward the garden but, not being able to see through her sweatshirt, she ran smack into the wall next to the gate.

"Wait a minute!" said the especially ugly guard, closing in on them.

"Yeah," said the regularly ugly guard. "Let us open that for you."

And they opened the gate and let them in.

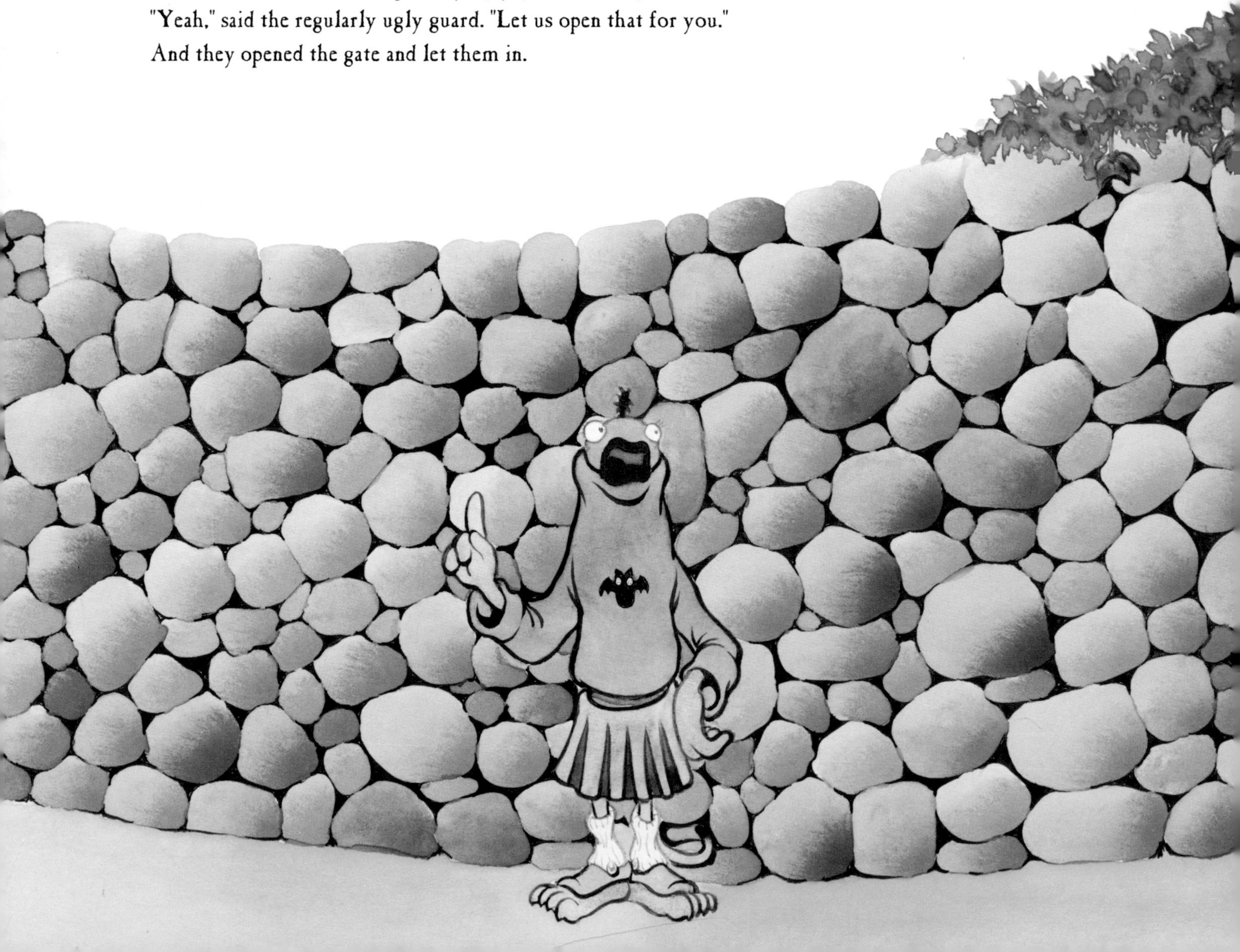

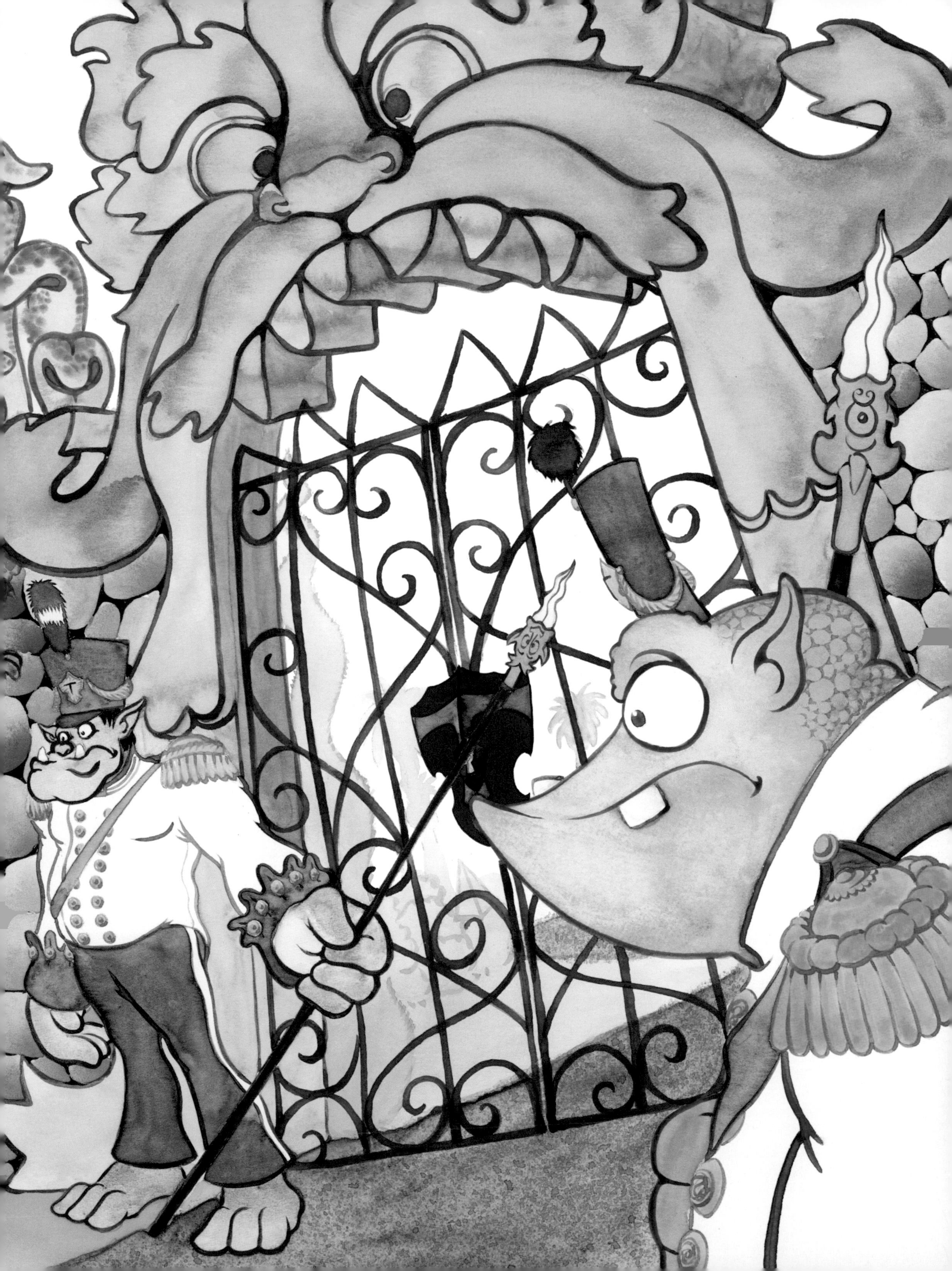

Once they had made it past the display of giant wartflowers and out of the guards' sight, Eppie jumped down off of Terrabella's head, and they began running through the garden.

"Fling! — That was great!" said Eppie as they ran past the globapple trees and fickleberry bushes.

"It did get us in, luckily," said Terrabella as she ran, "but how do we get out? Those walls are pretty tall."

"See, there!" said Eppie as they came racing around a fountain bubbling blobs of pond-scum. "We'll climb as quickly as a monkeyspider — cronk! — over the wall using those vines and. . . . "

Terrabella halted, looking back at Eppie who had stopped talking. Eppie had also stopped running and, for that matter, had stopped moving at all.

"What's wrong?" asked Terrabella.

"Shhhhhh!" said Eppie, pointing at the ground. Terrabella noticed they were standing right in the middle of dozens of holes.

Eppie's eyes were wide with alarm. "Sneeze weasels!" she whispered.

"Sneeze weasels?" whispered Terrabella, hearing faint sniffles coming from the holes.

"Yes," said Eppie, nodding, "They're to keep trespassers out of the garden. If we start them sneezing, we'll be caught for sure. We must be very quiet."

They tiptoed as quietly as they could, but Eppie seemed to be in a great deal of pain. Her face was scrunched up and she was whimpering.

"What's wrong?" whispered Terrabella, her eyes darting around the sea of sniffling holes.

"I don't want to yell out any of my favorite words," replied Eppie. "I should be all right as long as I don't think of any really good — FLIBBERTIGIBBET!!!"

The instant the word left her mouth, the ground exploded in a riot of sneezing sneeze weasels. They shot out of their holes propelled wildly into the air by the force of their sneezes. Zigzagging up and down and all around, the sneeze weasels made an utterly fantastic racket.

"*Ah-CHOO! Ah-CHOO! Ah-CHOO! Ah-CHOO! Ah-CHOO! Ah-CHOO! Ah-CHOO! Ah-CHOO!*" said the sneezing sneeze weasels.

"Stop right there!" said the very ugly and very, very ugly guards.

"Oh, no!" said a very sad Terrabella.

"Sorry," said a very sorry Eppie.

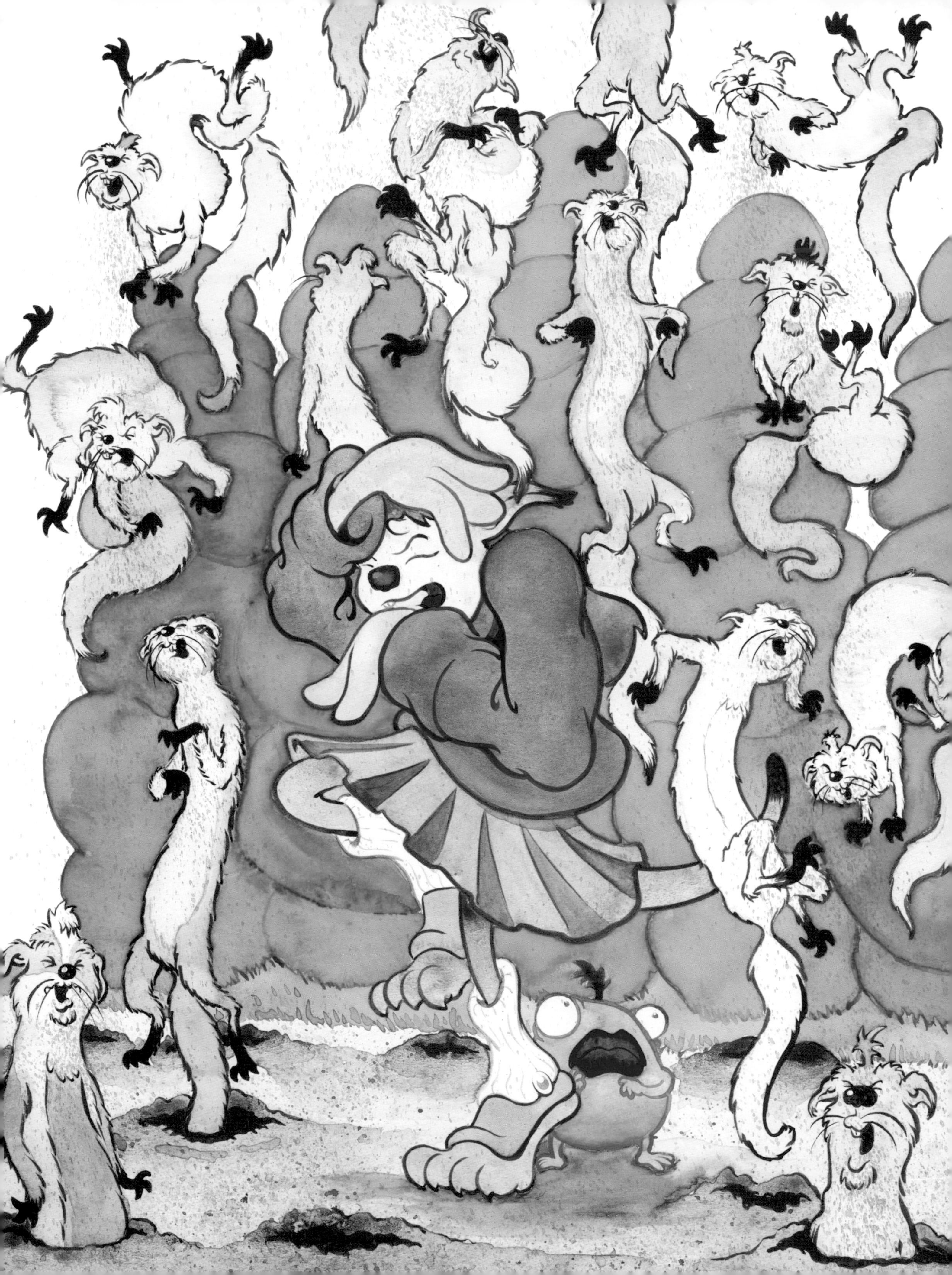

The guards swiftly marched Terrabella and Eppie into Ghastly Castle. Even though it was done up in brightly-colored "Monster of the Year" decorations, the overwhelming hugeness of the palace made Terrabella nervous.

"Mr. Guard, sir," asked Terrabella politely, "where are we going?"

"Me think you mean 'who are we going?'" replied the uglier guard.

"No, she's right," said the less ugly guard. "She means 'where are we going?'"

"Oh, all right then," said the uglier guard, looking more confused than usual, if that were possible. "You're going to . . . be quiet since it's none of your business! You'll find out soon enough."

As they were taken up several flights of stairs and through long corridors, Eppie realized where they were going. "I think — snip! — they're taking us to see Lord Thonk," she said. "This is the way to his chambers."

Although you might find it odd, Terrabella perked up at this news. Surely Lord Thonk would understand that the two of them were just a lost little girl and a harmless Dipp. Once he heard their story, she knew everything would get straightened out and she'd quickly be reunited with her family.

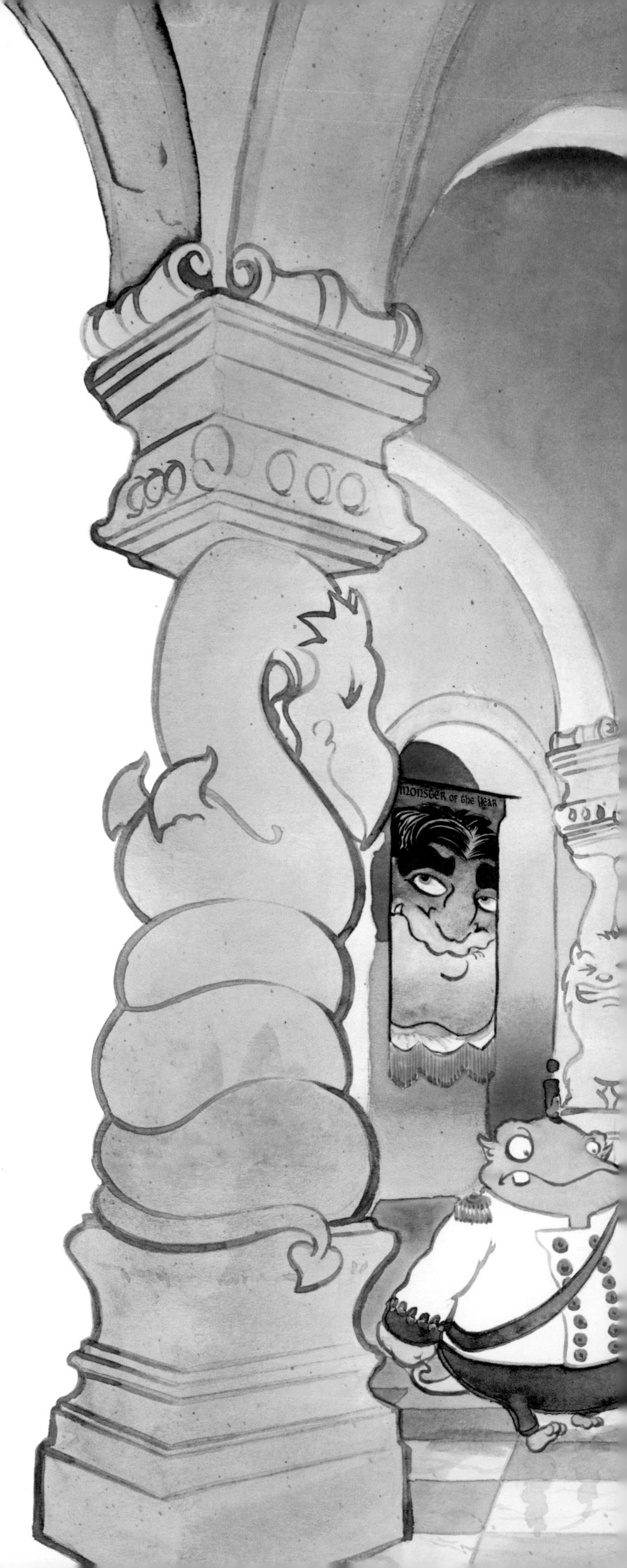
Monster of the Year

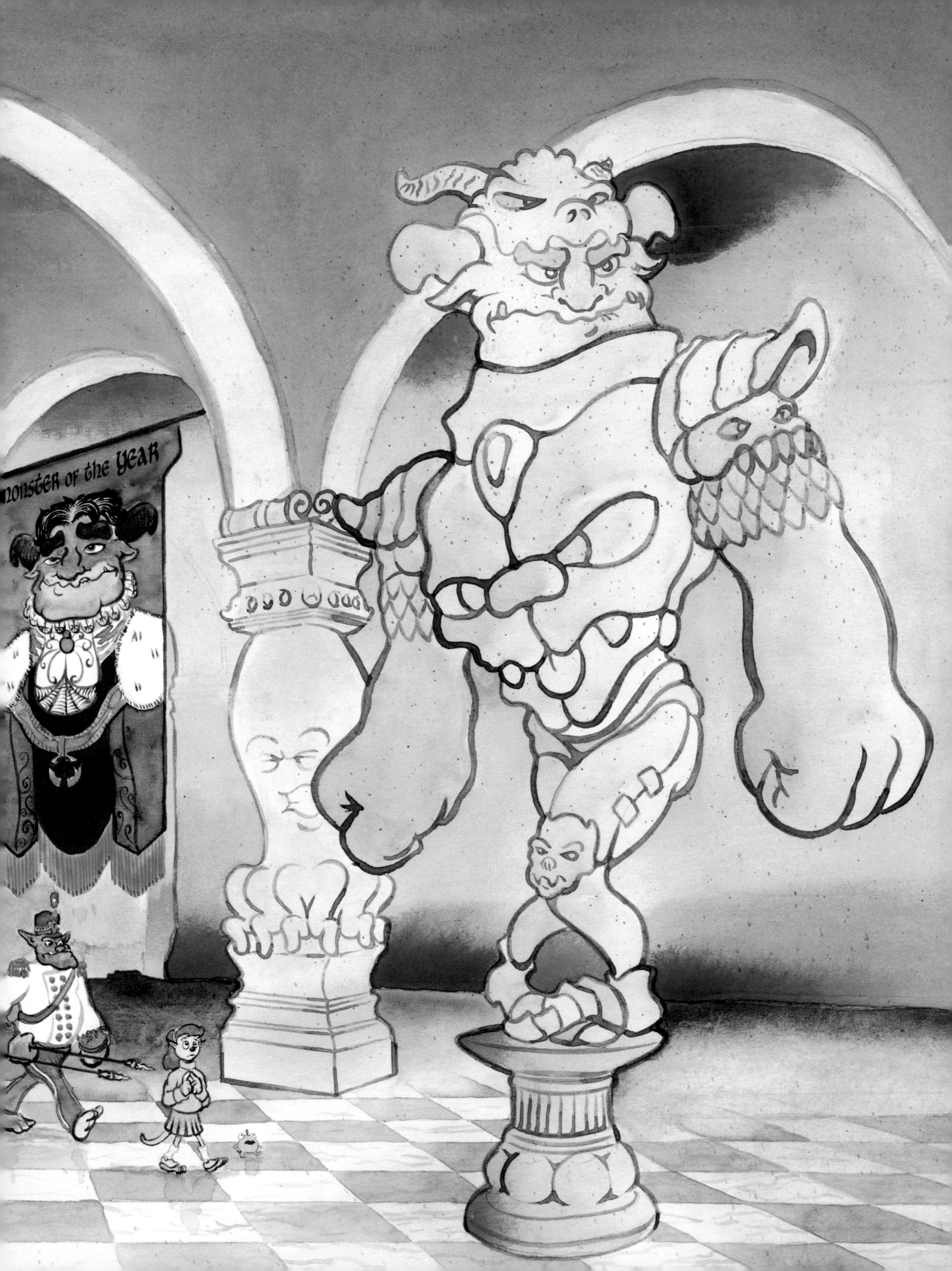

ONSTER OF the YEAR

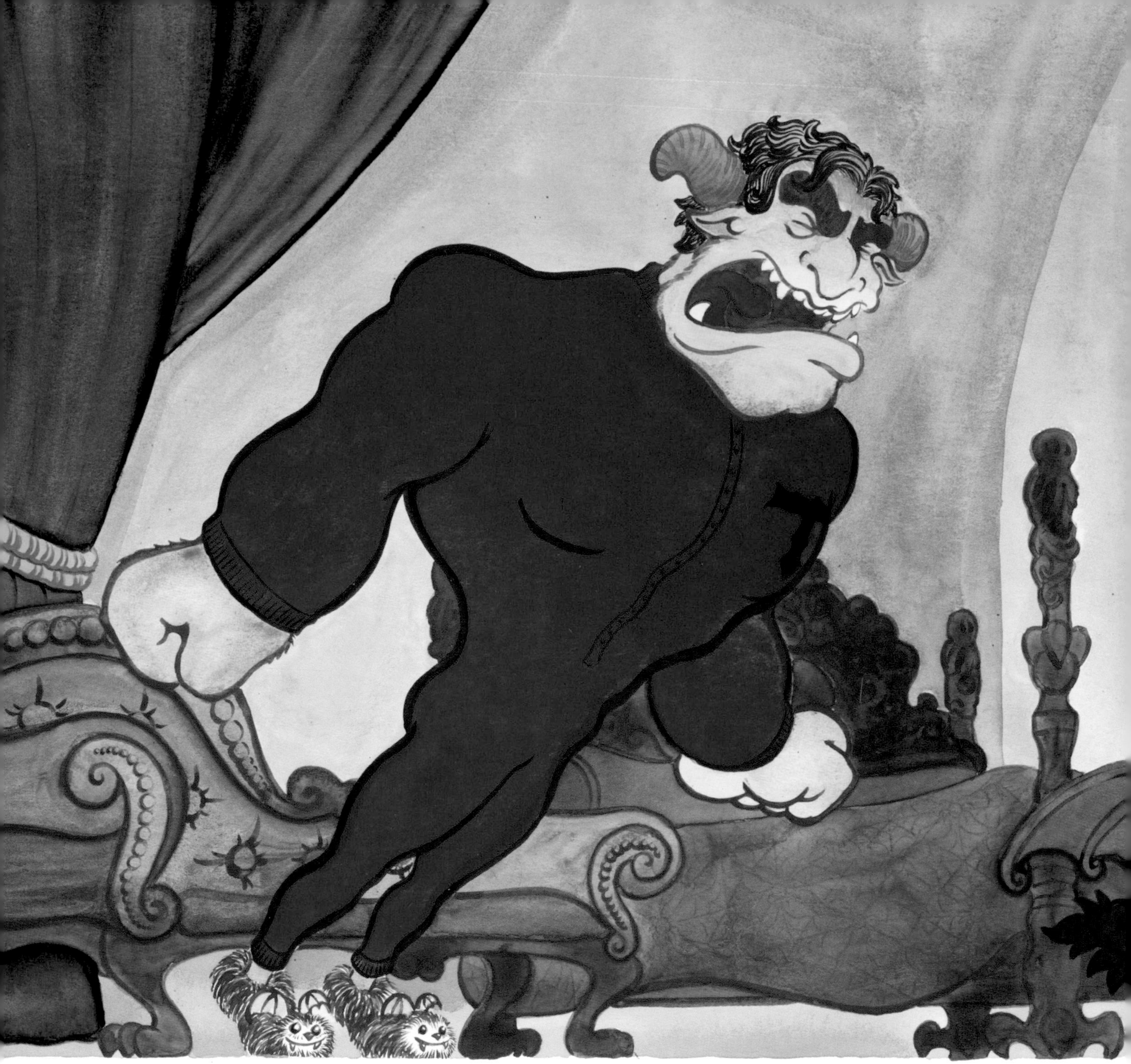

However, Lord Thonk was not at all happy to see them.

"I said throw them in the dungeon!" bellowed Lord Thonk as he hopped around in what seemed to be extreme rage. He crossed the room, looming over the four of them and looking as if he might very well explode. He pointed a huge finger at the guard who had presented the captured Eppie and Terrabella to him.

"You dare to barge in here," he growled, "on the day that I, Lord Thonk the Ghastly, am to be named Monster of the Year, merely to ask me what to do with these two phony plant inspectors?! Are you completely thick in the head?!!"

"Yes, sir, I am," said the ugly guard. "It's why you hired me, sir. Along with being really large and as dumb as two and half boxes of really stupid rocks."

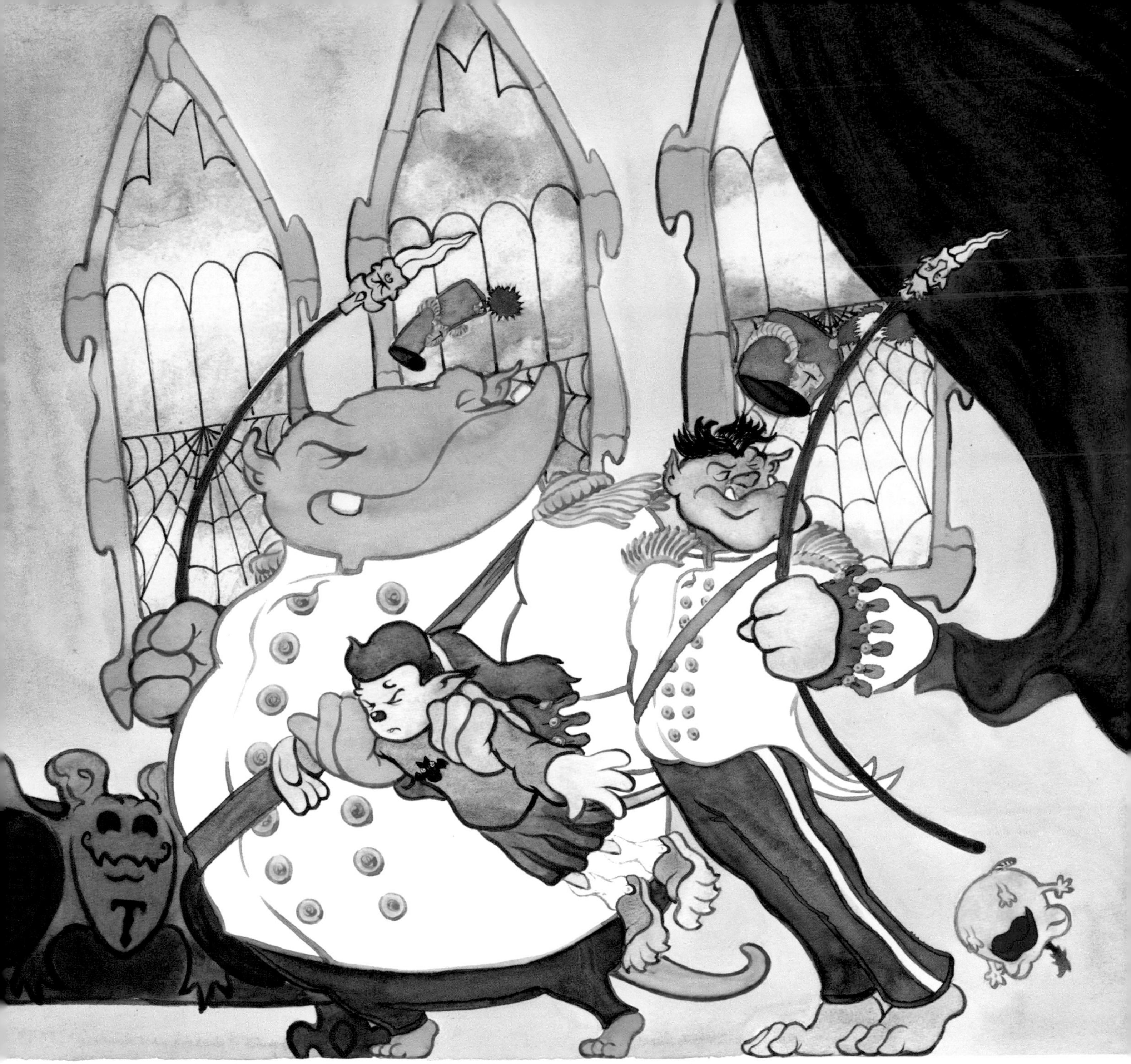

"Yup, I also! Dumb, dumb, dumb, dumb, dumb . . . and big!" agreed the uglier guard, smiling proudly at his big dumbness.

Terrabella could tell by the way Lord Thonk had stopped yelling and just stood shaking his clenched fists that he had indeed hired the two guards more for their large size than for their brains. However, before Terrabella could humbly introduce herself or explain their plight, Lord Thonk started yelling again.

"Enough!" cried Lord Thonk, looking uncomfortably mad. "I have no time for this ridiculousness! Take these two to the dungeon and toss them in a cage! Now, get out!"

"Yes, your Ghastliness!" said both the guards at the same time and, grabbing Terrabella and Eppie, they quickly ran out of the room.

Chapter Three: In The Dungeon

And so, Eppie and Terrabella were taken to Ghastly Castle's damp and dreary dungeon and locked up tight.

Terrabella slumped down in the corner of their cage, feeling the cold metal bars through her sweatshirt. She was very sad and now missed her family more than ever.

Eppie, on the other hand, was extra double mad and shook the cage bars with all her tiny might. "You let us out of here! We — gibberish! — haven't done anything bad!" she yelled to no one in particular.

Then a voice from the gloom said, "There's no use in making all that noise, Eppie. You know how Lord Thonk dislikes babbling."

"Mr. Maladee, is that you?" Eppie squinted into the dungeon's darkness.

Terrabella was taken aback by the fact that Eppie seemed to know the owner of the voice. She was also surprised to see, as her eyes started adjusting to the gray gloom, that Mr. Maladee was not the only other guest in the dungeon. There were dozens of cages of varying sizes, all holding sad-looking monsters.

"Do you know these monsters?" Terrabella whispered to Eppie.

Eppie squinched up her eyes and looked around. "Yes!" she said in a surprised voice. "I know all of them!"

Terrabella stood to introduce herself. "My name is Terrabella Smoot," she said, peering up through the bars at the kindly looking figure in the cage above her. "Mr. Maladee, how do you know Eppie? Who are you?"

"I am the head of staff," replied Mr. Maladee, "and these are all the servants of Ghastly Castle."

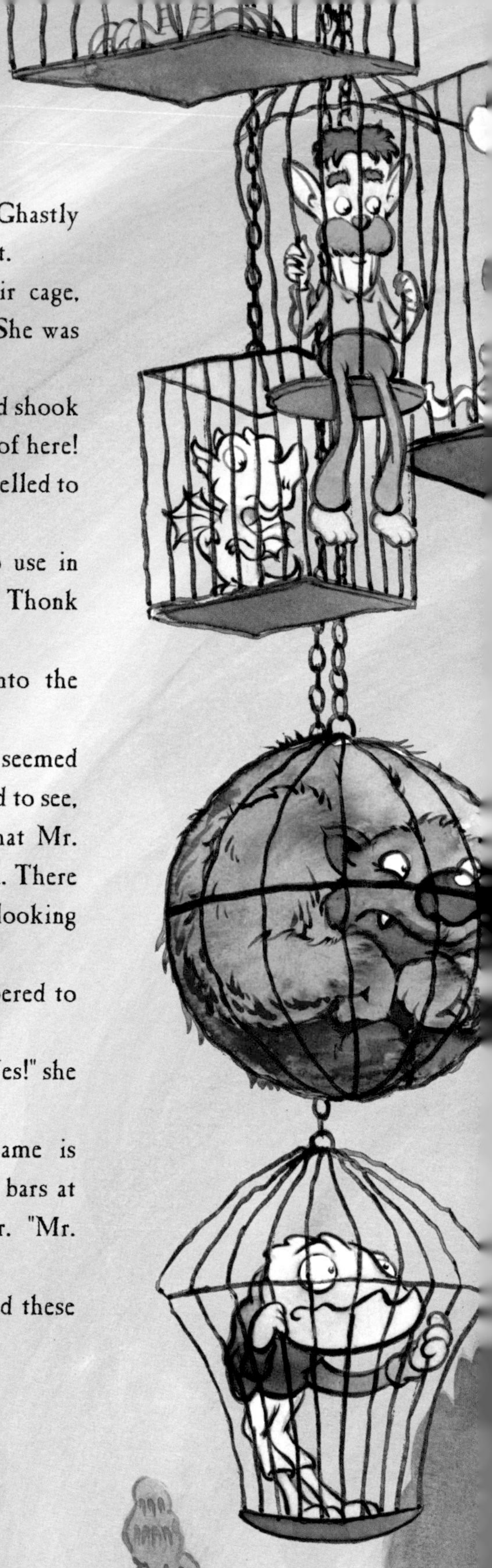

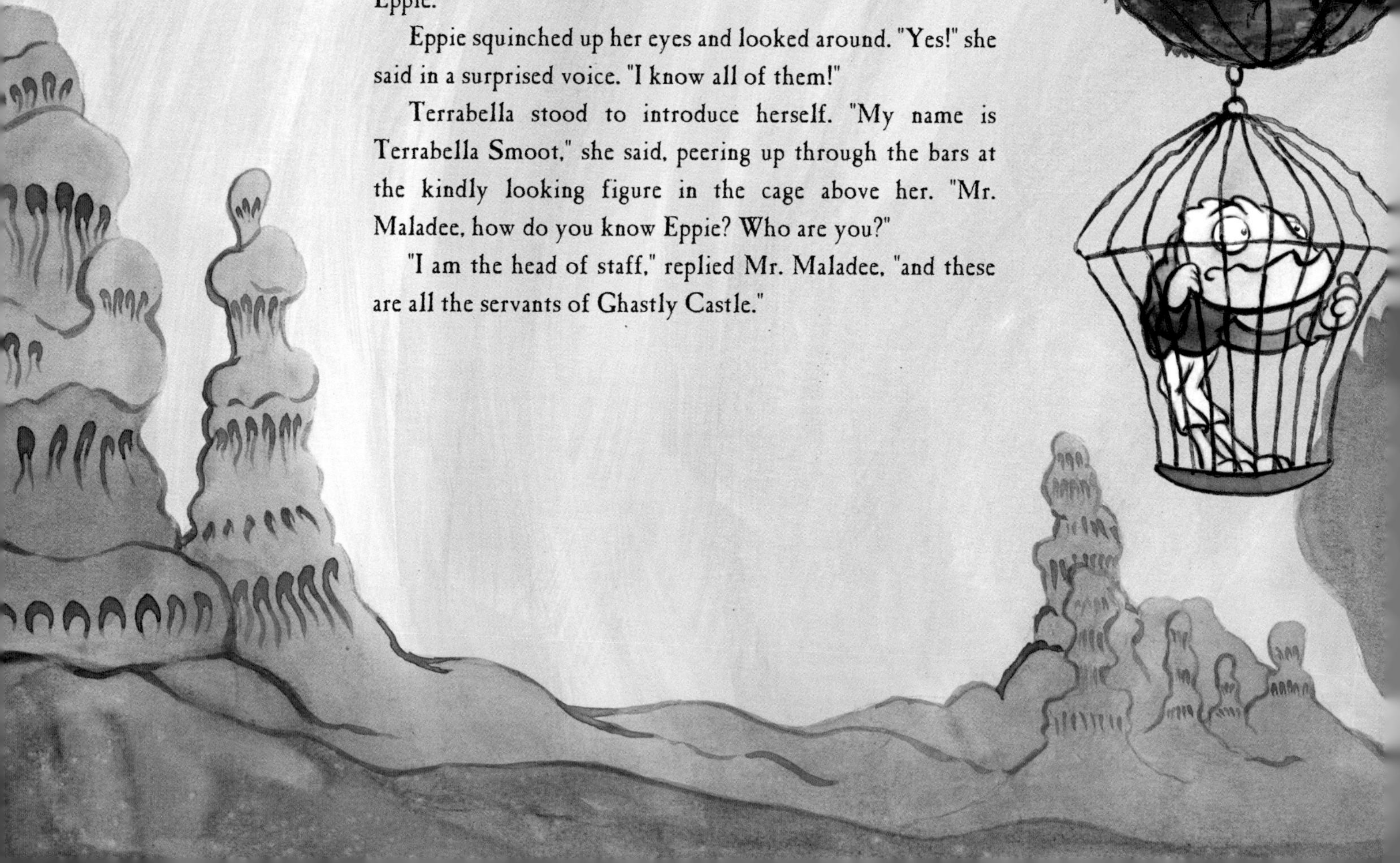

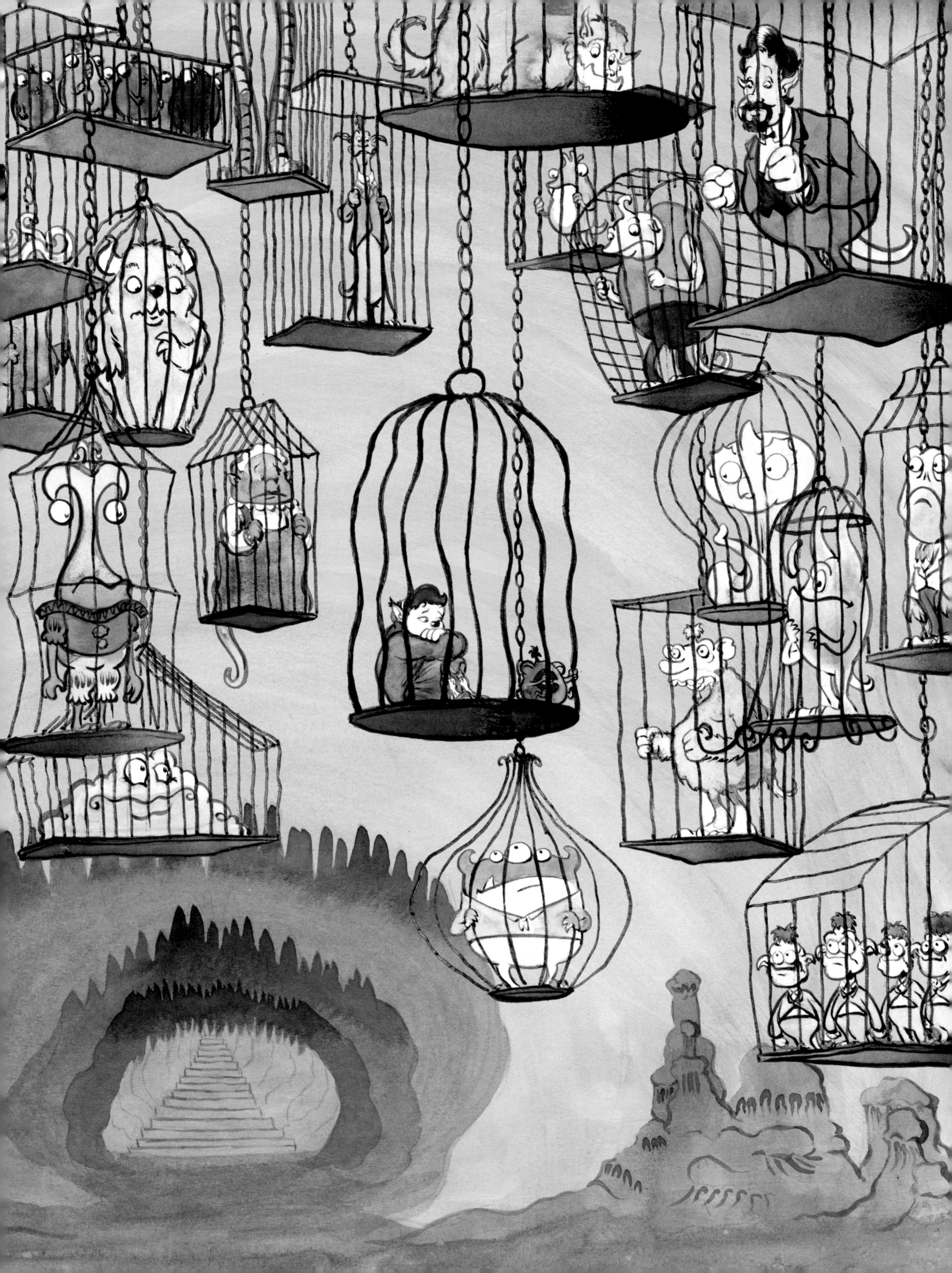

"Shouldn't you be at the Monster of the Year celebration?" asked Terrabella. "Why are you all in the dungeon?"

"Lord Thonk said that it was for our own good," replied Mr. Maladee.

"Why?" asked Terrabella. "Are you nasty beasties who eat small children? Or maybe Lord Thonk can see into the future and knows you'll do something bad or . . . ?"

"We have done nothing but our jobs," interrupted Mr. Maladee politely. There was a murmur of agreement among the other monsters.

"Well, what are your jobs?" asked Terrabella.

One by one, the monsters told Terrabella how they served in Ghastly Castle. Some cooked, some did chores like making sure the spider webs were hung just right or that there was a nice layer of dust on the shelves or that the rooms were properly dank -- things you would expect from the staff of a large castle.

A few had very specific jobs, like taking care of all the rare and dangerous beasties in Lord Thonk's zoo or hitting Lord Thonk regularly with the Ugly Stick so he could keep up his youthful repulsiveness or inspecting the plants in the royal garden.

"And what do you do?" Terrabella asked the last member of Ghastly Castle's staff.

"I'd rather not say," said the nervous-looking monster. "I might get in trouble."

"More trouble than being locked in a dungeon?" asked Terrabella.

"I guess you're right," sighed the monster. Then he whispered, "I build bathrooms."

"You build bathrooms?" replied a puzzled Terrabella.

"Yes, thirty-seven so far," said the monster. "You see, Lord Thonk has a very, very tiny bladder. He has to visit a bathroom every fifteen minutes."

"Every fifteen minutes?" asked Terrabella. "Then how could he have thumb-wrestled Goflarb the Giant for three days straight? Or hunted the Wild Bugbear of Blarm for weeks before capturing it? Or go through the Super Slimy Swamp to get the Very Interesting Tea Set from the Western Witches?"

The dungeon fell silent as everyone tried to think of how Lord Thonk could have possibly done all his mighty deeds, the deeds for which he would be named Monster of the Year that very night, if he had a bladder weaker than a Yellow-Striped Pipsqueaker.

The answer was that he hadn't done any of these great deeds at all.

"The Wild Bugbear of Blarm," said one monster, "was part of a traveling circus. Lord Thonk bought it, cage and all, and hired me on as its trainer."

Another said, "He sent me to get the Very Interesting Tea Set in a small shop in Glumbug Village."

Monster after monster told of deeds that Lord Thonk had claimed as his own that they had done for him. It was only now, in the dungeon, that they felt safe enough to tell the others.

"I'm afraid we need to escape," said Mr. Maladee. "Who knows what Lord Thonk will do to us to keep his secrets after he's been made Monster of the Year."

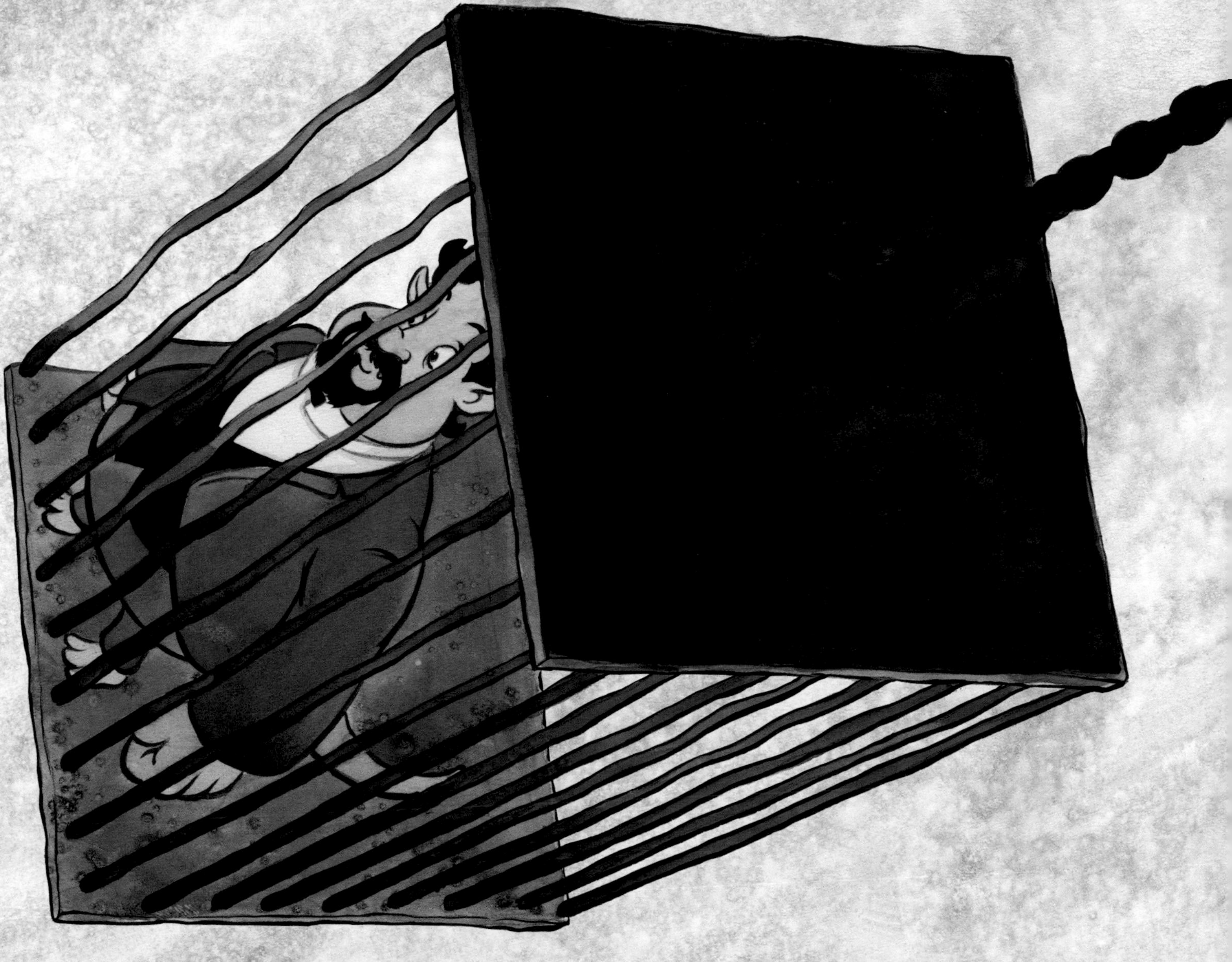

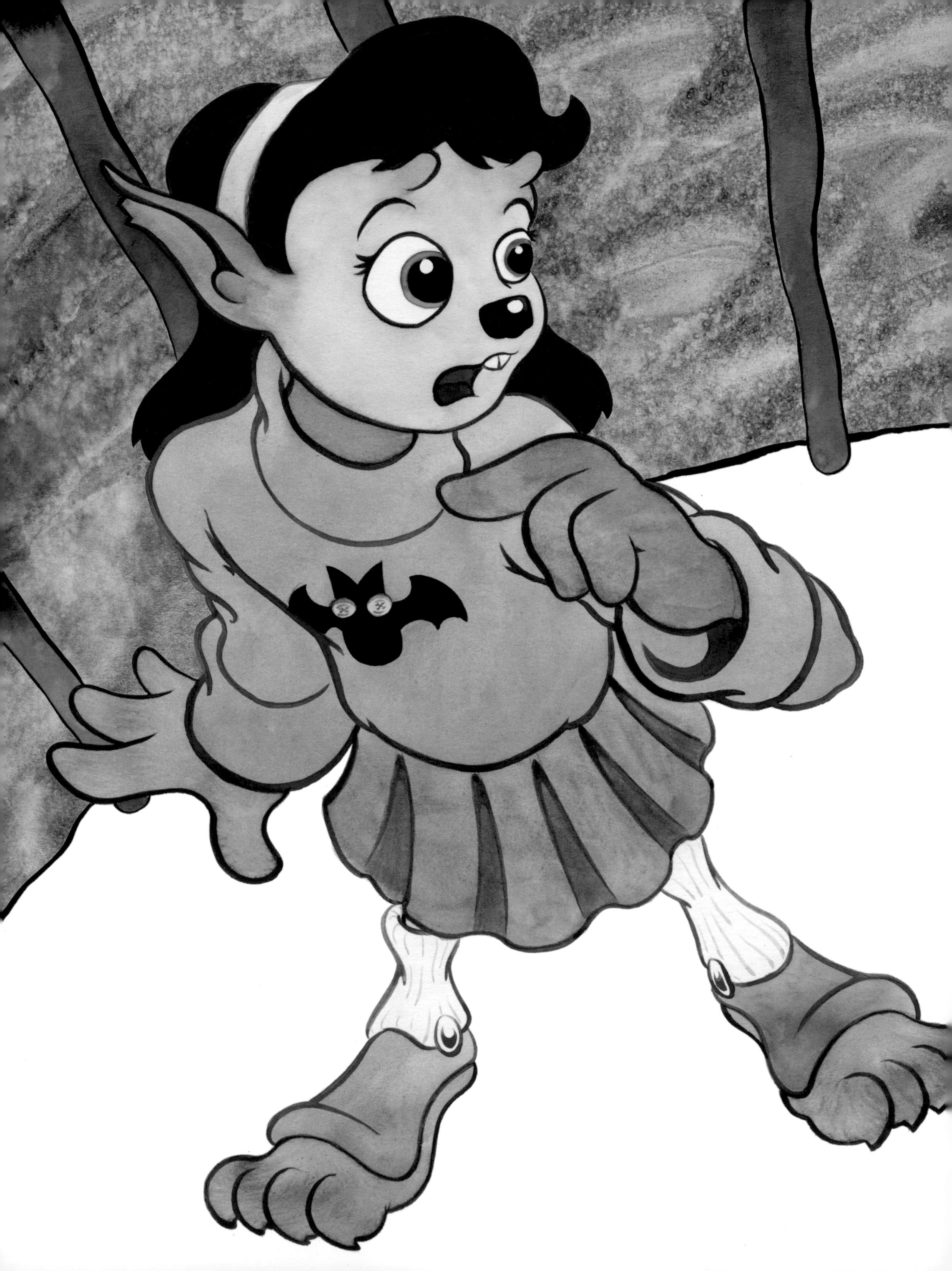

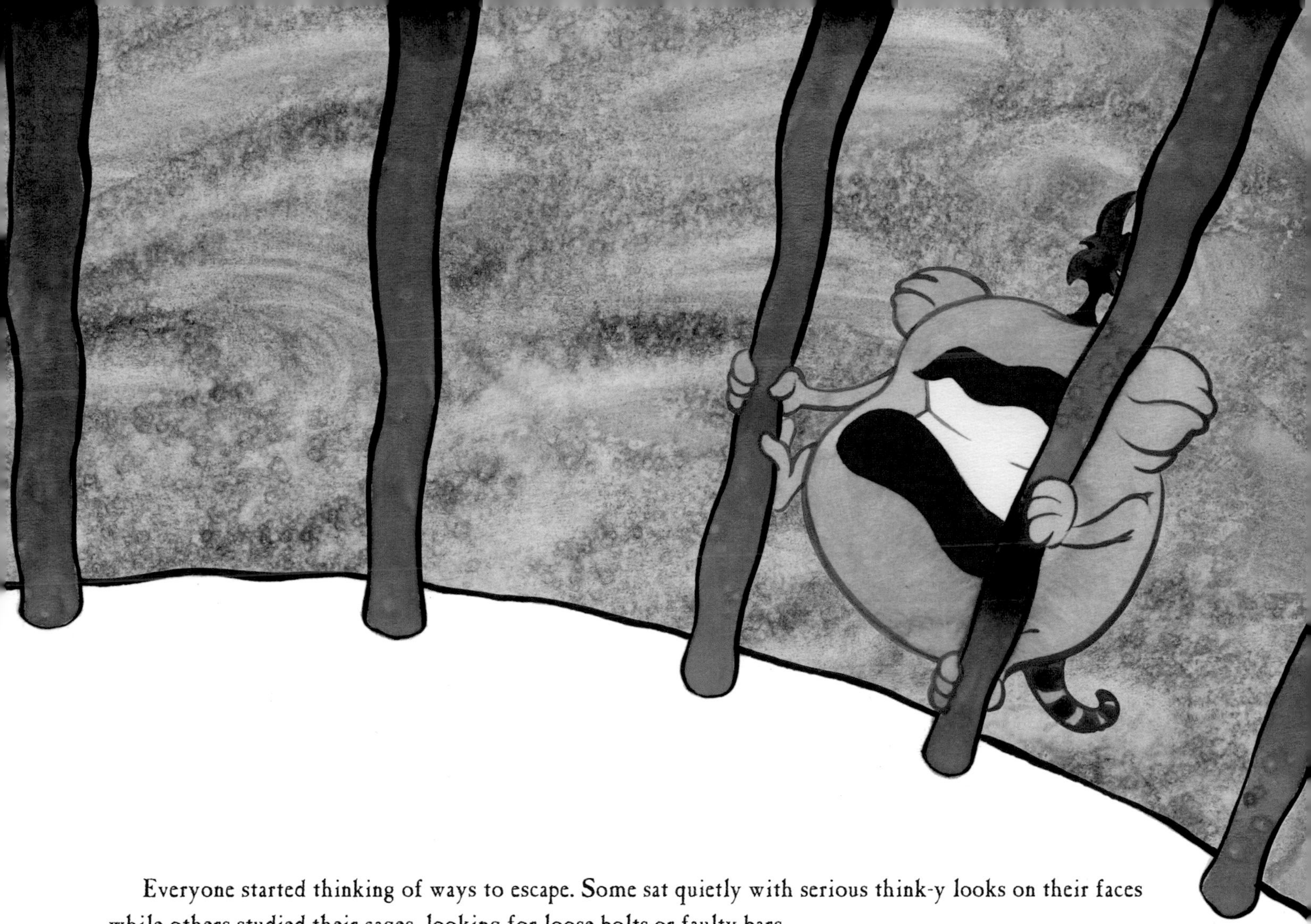

Everyone started thinking of ways to escape. Some sat quietly with serious think-y looks on their faces while others studied their cages, looking for loose bolts or faulty bars.

Eppie went back to her original plan, violently shaking the cage door.

"Open — codswallop! — you silly thing!" she said loudly as she shook away.

"I don't think that's going to work," said Terrabella, who had been trying hard to think.

"Maybe if — ruckus! — I try it from the other side," replied Eppie. She squeezed through the bars and started shaking the cage door from the outside.

"Eppie!" cried Terrabella.

Eppie jumped at the sound of her name and scrambled back through the bars. "What?" she asked anxiously.

"You fit through the bars! You can escape!" said Terrabella.

"Oh! You're right!" said Eppie.

Mr. Maladee instantly knew what to do and gave instructions. "Eppie," he said, "we need you to set us free. Just go up those stairs to the dungeon control room and spin the wheel that lowers and opens the cages. The guard comes by every twenty minutes, so you'll have to work as fast as you can, all right?"

"Yes, sir!" said Eppie. She squeezed through the bars again, jumped to the dungeon floor and took off running up the stairs.

"Wait!" Terrabella called after her. Eppie skidded to a stop. "If you think of any of your favorite words, please say them quietly."

"Gotcha!" said Eppie, giving Terrabella a salute. "I'll be back lickitysplit! Ooo, that's a good one — lickitysplit!" She clamped her hands over her mouth and looked terribly guilty.

"Sorry," Eppie said and ran from the room, leaving a trail of whispered nifty words and a dungeon full of doubtful monsters.

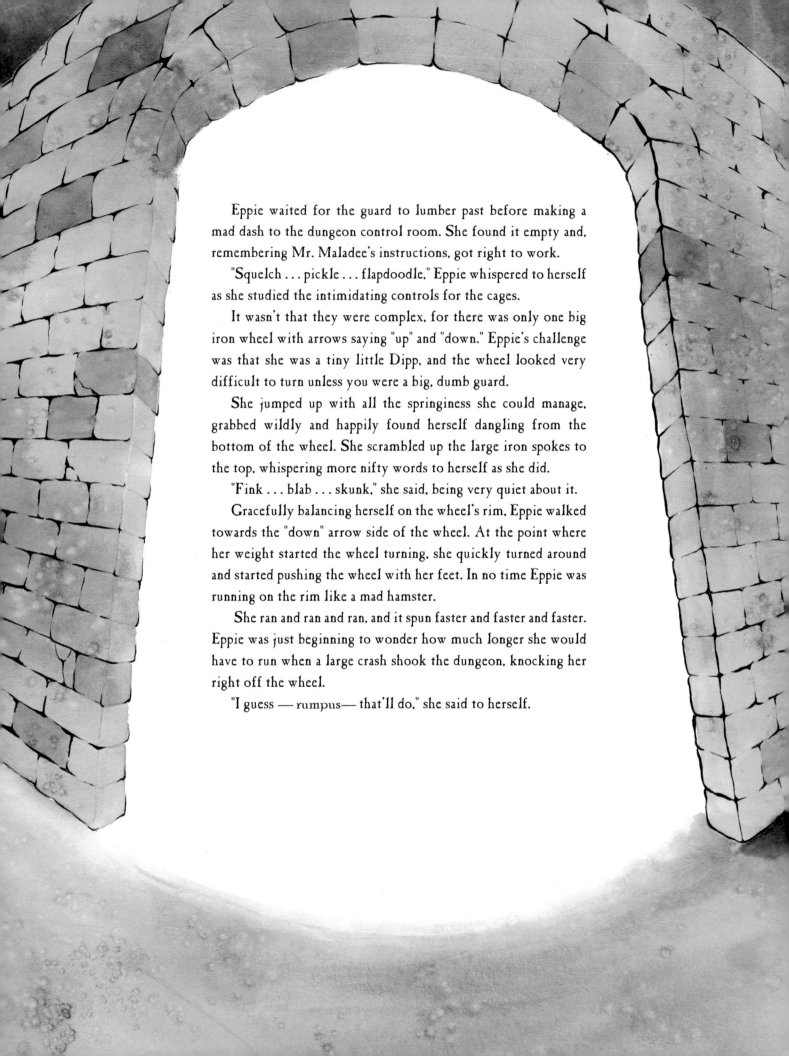

Eppie waited for the guard to lumber past before making a mad dash to the dungeon control room. She found it empty and, remembering Mr. Maladee's instructions, got right to work.

"Squelch . . . pickle . . . flapdoodle," Eppie whispered to herself as she studied the intimidating controls for the cages.

It wasn't that they were complex, for there was only one big iron wheel with arrows saying "up" and "down." Eppie's challenge was that she was a tiny little Dipp, and the wheel looked very difficult to turn unless you were a big, dumb guard.

She jumped up with all the springiness she could manage, grabbed wildly and happily found herself dangling from the bottom of the wheel. She scrambled up the large iron spokes to the top, whispering more nifty words to herself as she did.

"Fink . . . blab . . . skunk," she said, being very quiet about it.

Gracefully balancing herself on the wheel's rim, Eppie walked towards the "down" arrow side of the wheel. At the point where her weight started the wheel turning, she quickly turned around and started pushing the wheel with her feet. In no time Eppie was running on the rim like a mad hamster.

She ran and ran and ran, and it spun faster and faster and faster. Eppie was just beginning to wonder how much longer she would have to run when a large crash shook the dungeon, knocking her right off the wheel.

"I guess — rumpus— that'll do," she said to herself.

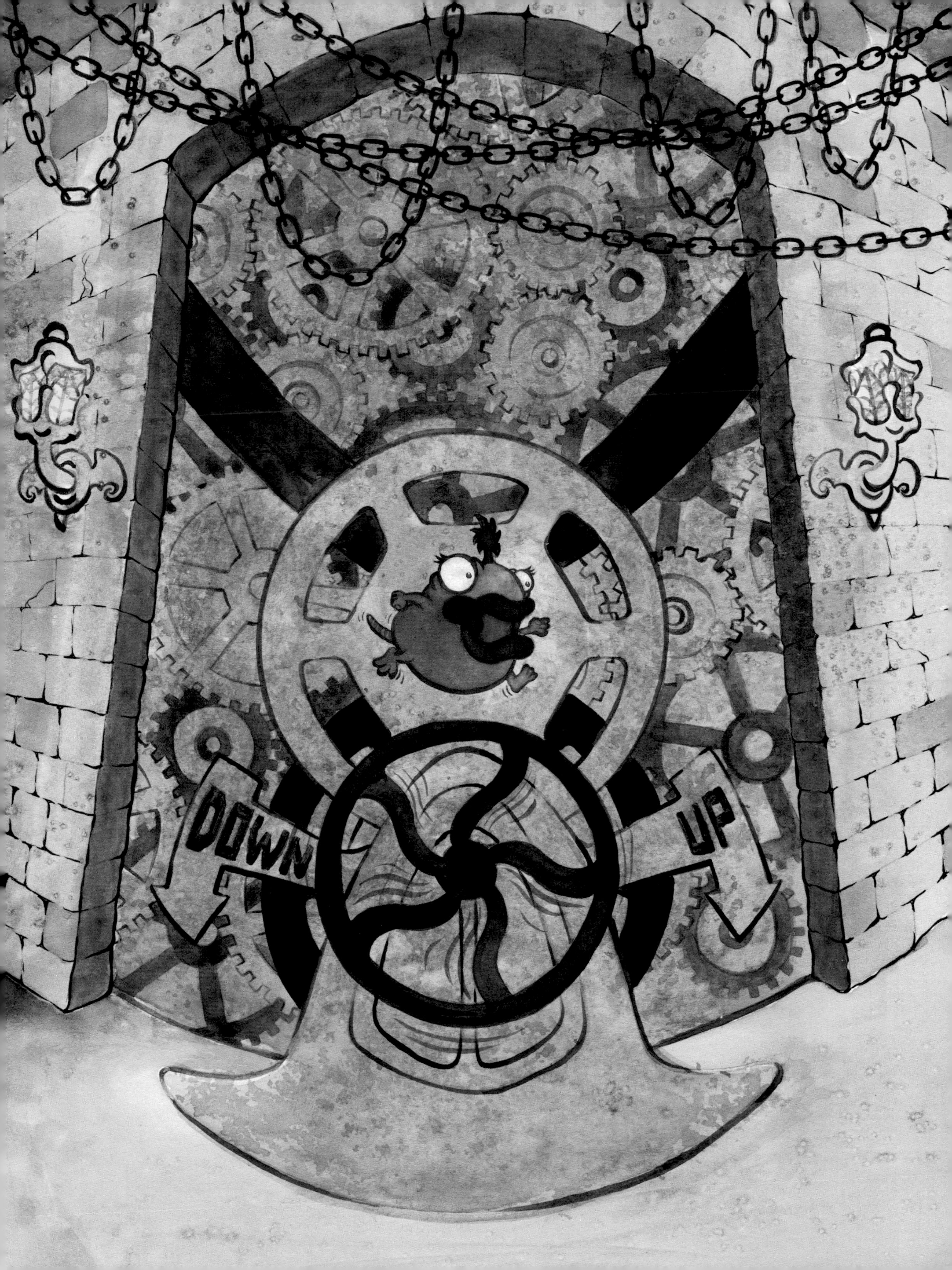
DOWN
UP

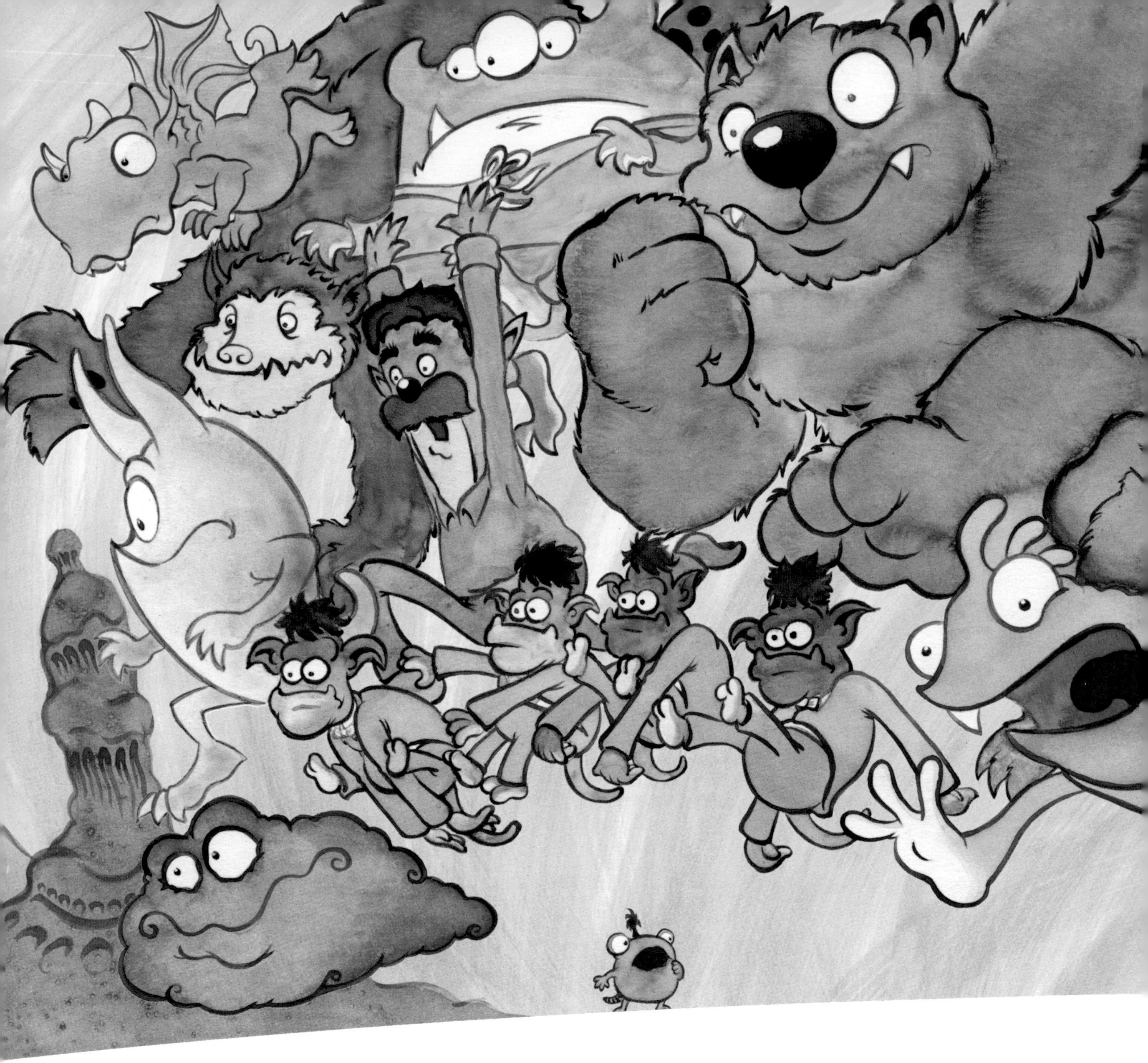

Eppie scurried back to the dungeon to find that she had done well; the cages were all on the ground and open. However, everyone in them looked like they had been dropped quite unexpectedly.

"I probably should have mentioned that you should turn the wheel slowly," said Mr. Maladee, rubbing his head as he came out of his cage. "But you made quick work of it, and for that I'm grateful."

Eppie was a bit embarrassed by her mistake, but having been freed, everyone seemed happy. In fact, the mood in the dungeon seemed almost cheerful, with the monsters thanking Eppie as they stretched their formerly imprisoned limbs.

That is, until Terrabella piped up, "Now we can all go stop Lord Thonk from becoming Monster of the Year!"

The dungeon went silent and the monsters darted nervous looks at each other.

"I'm sorry, my dear," said Mr. Maladee. "I think it best that we all run away from here very quickly and never look back. In fact, I'm going to run away right now." And, having said that, he dashed at a breakneck pace up the stairs, flung open the dungeon door and disappeared into the night.

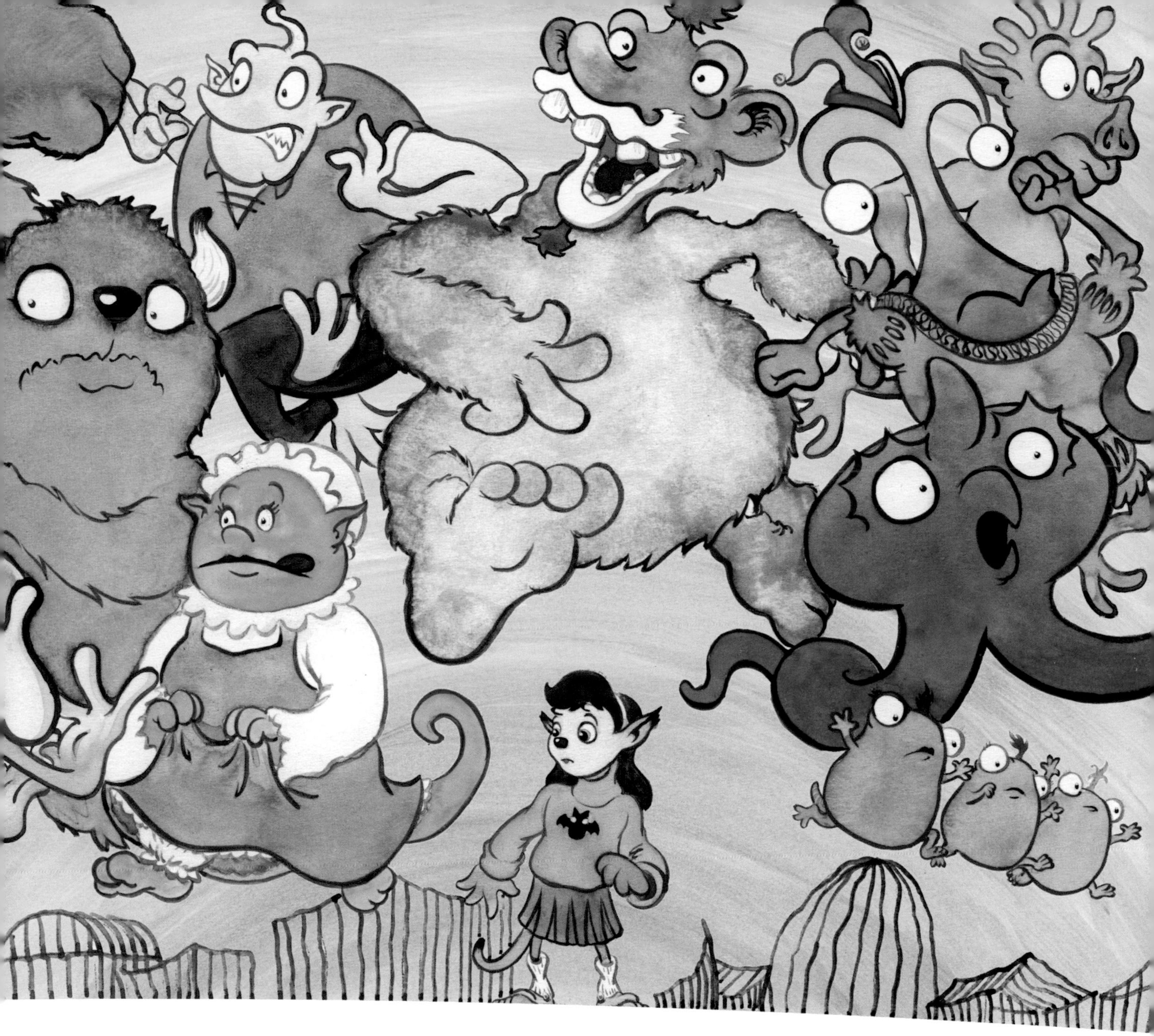

Terrabella turned around to find that the other monsters wouldn't meet her eyes. "You all know it's not fair for him to become Monster of the Year, don't you?" she pleaded.

But even as they nodded in agreement, a few started inching towards the door, then more of them, then finally they all ran past Terrabella like a herd of frightened mildewbeasts.

Terrabella saw that Eppie hadn't started running like the rest, but she did have a very troubled look on her face. Terrabella looked hopefully at Eppie, her steady friend through this entire miserable adventure.

Eppie looked at Terrabella and opened her mouth but, unbelievably, she seemed to have nothing to say. Finally, Eppie just turned and ran away, the last monster through the dungeon door.

"If you don't stop him, I will!" Terrabella called desperately, but her cry just echoed in the empty dungeon.

For the second time that day, Terrabella found herself totally alone. Tears welled up in her eyes as she thought of all the really crummy things that had happened on a day that was supposed to have been magnificently wonderful. Then, between sniffles, she heard the distant sound of trumpets.

The Monster of the Year celebration was beginning.

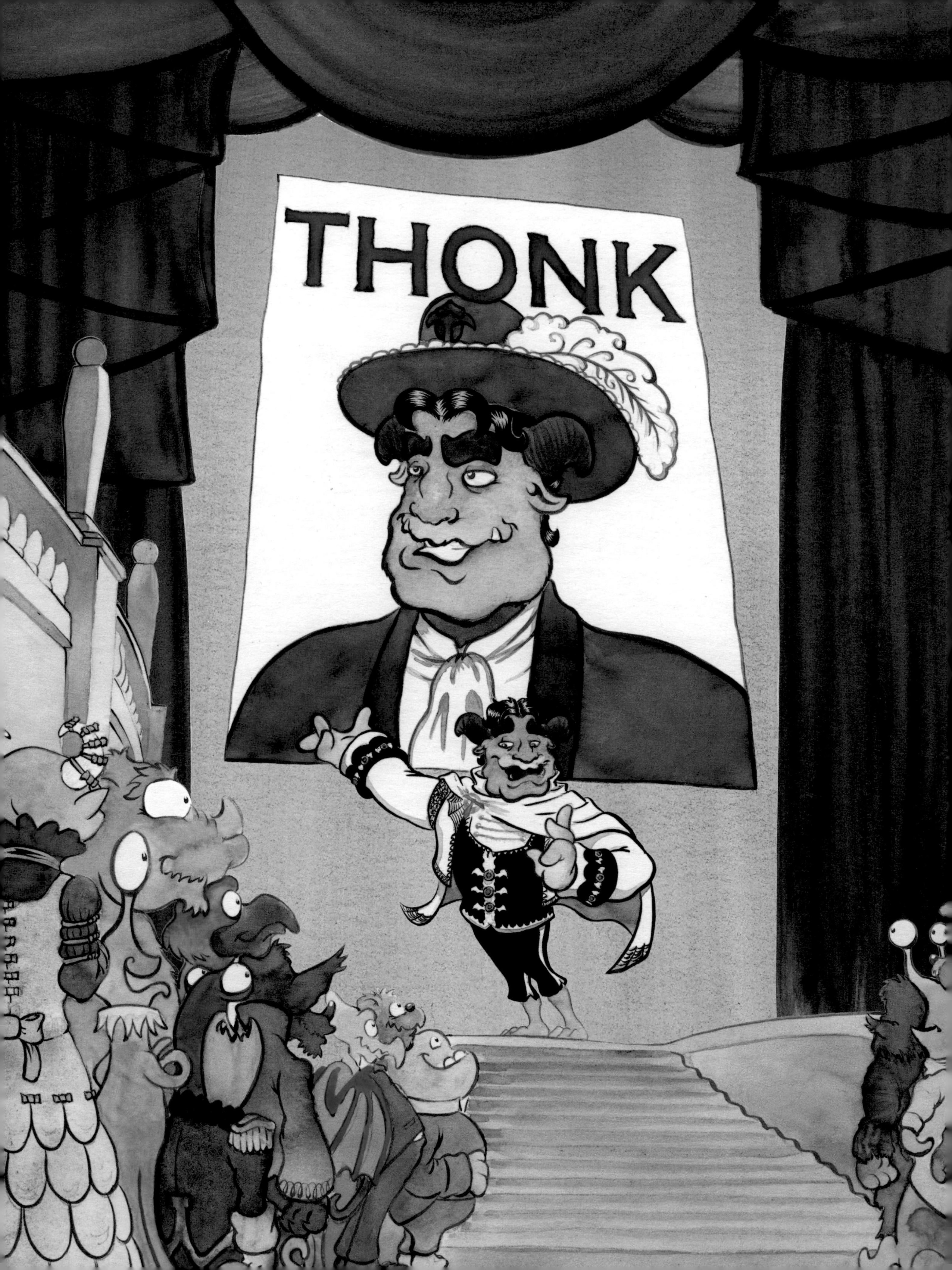
THONK

Chapter Four: Monster of the Year

Terrabella forced back her tears, wiped her nose and set off up the stairs into the heart of the castle - both to stop Lord Thonk and to find her family.

She made her way through Ghastly Castle by taking advantage of the dimness of the stairwells, hallways and palace guards. After trudging up many a staircase she finally reached the Castle's great hall and the big celebration. As she snuck in, the huge crowd of monsters exploded in applause. For a moment Terrabella thought the cheering was for her, for being a brave little monster, but then Lord Thonk began to speak and she realized the applause had been for him all along.

"Dear, dear friends," said Lord Thonk in his booming voice, "I am so glad you could be here tonight for this grand evening of celebrating... me. I have always attempted to be the best monster I could be whether I was fighting giant beasties, questing for magical treasure or merely being devilishly ugly."

The crowd laughed and cheered at this and Lord Thonk gave them a smile and a wink in return.

"I am truly grateful," he continued, "for your affection and admiration of myself and my mighty deeds. You may not realize this, but being incredibly monstrous is quite hard work. When I'm out on a quest, I have only my stunning cunning and massive muscles to defeat giants, dragons and the occasional berserk troll.

"Why, even here in my own castle I have to be ever ready for an epic battle! Just today my elite guards were easily overpowered by two hulking brutes whose dastardly goal was nothing less than to ruin this celebration for all of you! Fortunately, as you can see by the fact that my magnificence stands before you now, I single-handedly took care of the despicable trespassers."

The audience cheered at hearing how their hero had been doing splendidly heroic things that very day. Terrabella did not cheer, however; she just fumed. She knew that the "hulking brutes" he was talking about were merely herself and Eppie.

Terrabella was so mad at Lord Thonk and she had heard enough! It was now or never! She opened her mouth to tell Lord Thonk a thing or two when a pair of hands reached out of the crowd and snatched her right up.

As her feet left the ground, Terrabella's stomach dropped. She knew for sure that she was doomed to make a return trip to the dungeon where she would spend the rest of her unlucky life.

At least, that's what she thought until she was spun around and given a big hug.

"There you are!" said Grandpa Smoot, "We've been looking for you all over Ghastliville! Your parents will be so happy I found you!"

"Mphhhmph!" said Terrabella as her grandfather joyously crushed her to his chest.

"Shhhhhh! Be quiet! Lord Thonk is speaking!" said several nearby monsters.

"Be quiet yourself!" said Grandpa Smoot right back at them. He set Terrabella down and glared at the shushers, seeming to dare them to say anything else that would spoil his reunion with his granddaughter.

Terrabella's emotions had become a big jumble. She was happy and relieved to have been found, proud of her grandfather for sticking up for them, but also very nervous that they were drawing too much attention to themselves. It was one thing for her to get in trouble for telling off Lord Thonk, but the thought of her grandfather getting thrown in the dungeon was too much for her.

"Grandpa!" she whispered, "We need to go before. . . ."

"YOU BE QUIET NOW!!" bellowed a guard who had appeared behind them from out of nowhere. "YOU NO TALK WHILE LORD THONK IS SPEACHING!!"

All the monsters in the great hall gasped at this rude interruption and everyone turned to see who would be on the wrong end of Lord Thonk's well-known temper. Those monsters near Terrabella and her grandfather backed away, not wanting to be associated with such ill-mannered troublemakers.

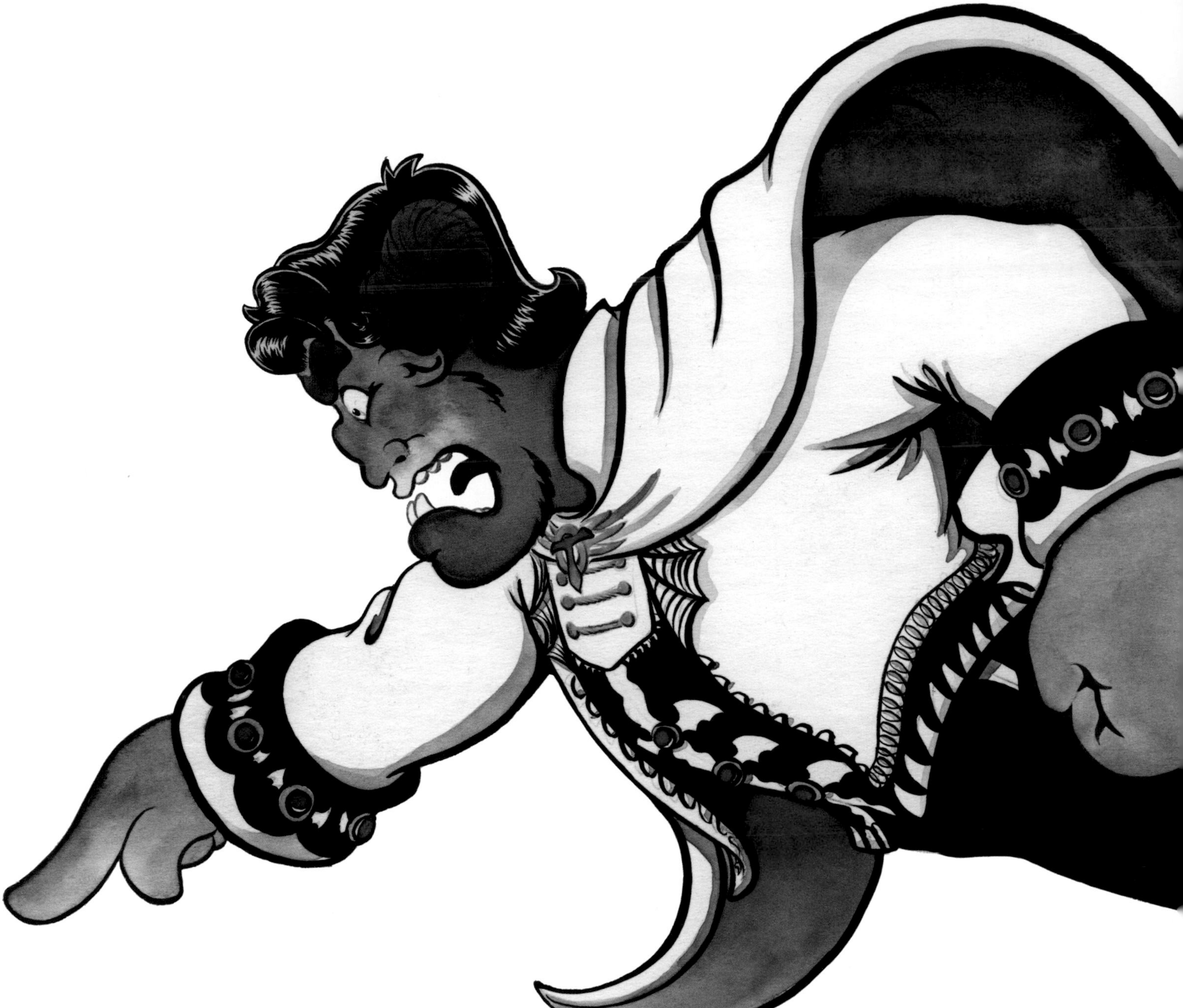

"You!" roared Lord Thonk, who had recognized Terrabella and was pointing squarely at her. "How dare you escape from my dungeon and attempt to upstage the world famous Lord Thonk! This is my night! This is all about me! I'm the Monster of the Year!"

"More like the Windbag of the Year, if you ask me," said a voice that Terrabella was quite surprised to hear.

Another huge gasp went up from the crowd, and everyone turned to look where this new outburst had come from. There, on the balcony was Mr. Maladee and all the unsung monsters.

Terrabella felt a tug on her skirt. It was Eppie!

"I convinced them — zowie! — to come back," she whispered.

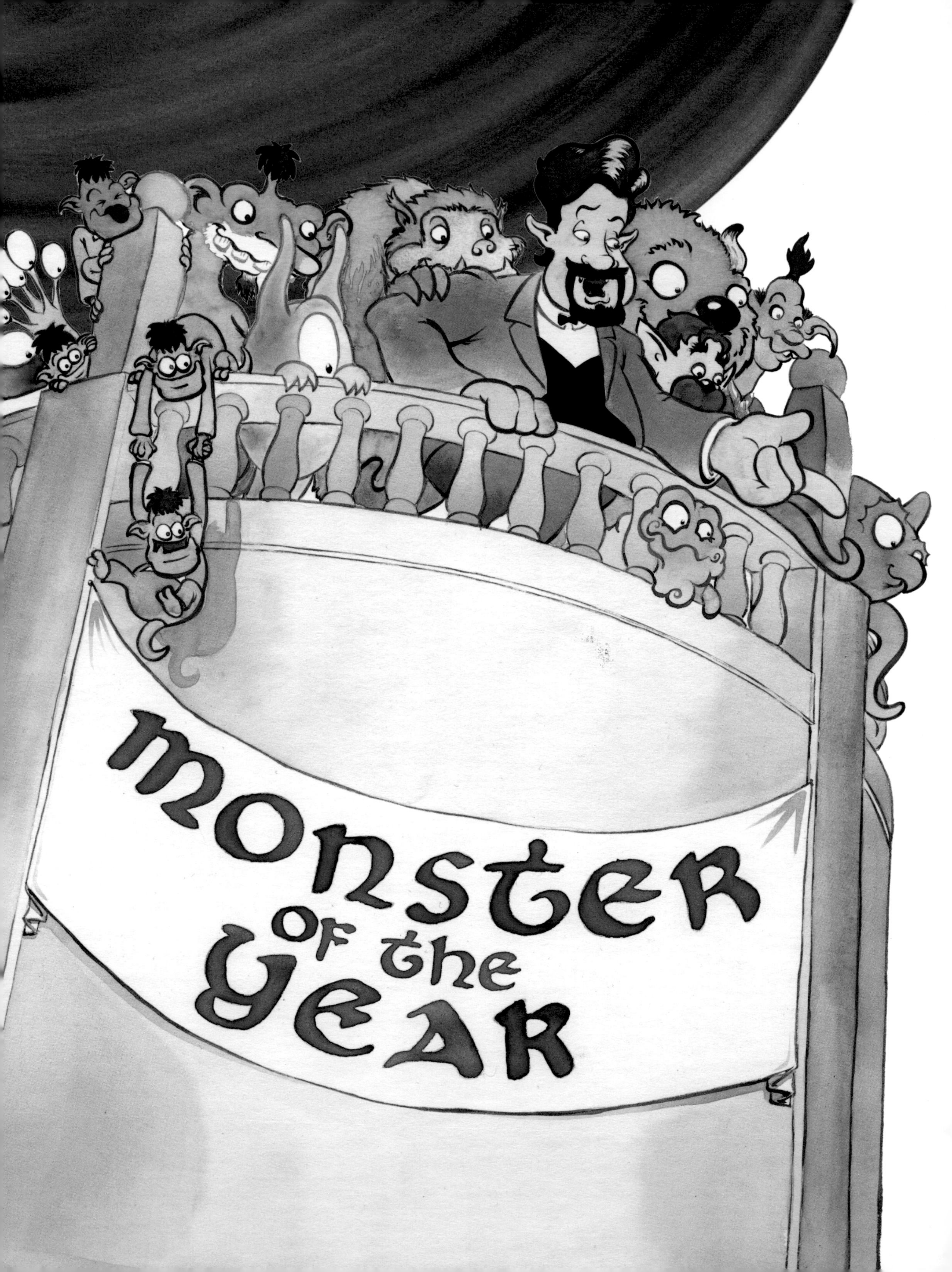
MONSTER
OF THE
YEAR

"Braft! Zillbit! Gizditch!" sputtered Lord Thonk, who was now so angry that he'd forgotten how to use real words.

"I haven't quite finished what I would like to say," interrupted Mr. Maladee. "We, the staff of Ghastly Castle, are here to inform everyone that it was we who did the work that has made you Monster of the Year!"

Again, there were more astonished gasps from the crowd.

"For years now," Mr. Maladee continued, "you've taken credit for our hard work, all because we were afraid of you. You bullied us, constantly yelled at us and even threw us in your dungeon, but tonight, we unsung monsters are here to stand up to you . . . all because of the bravery of one little girl. That girl right there!"

As Mr. Maladee pointed to Terrabella there were still more astonished gasps from the crowd, which was actually quite enjoying all the exciting astonishment. Terrabella blushed a little and waved shyly to the crowd.

"Hello," she said.

"Gentle monsters," Mr. Maladee continued, "I don't expect you to believe us without proof. So, now that I've talked for a good long time, we will let Lord Thonk tell you himself why he should be Monster of the Year. However, if for some reason, he cannot explain himself, then we offer that as proof that he is nothing more than a liar and a scoundrel.

"So, Lord Thonk," Mr. Maladee concluded, "what do you have to say for yourself?"

Lord Thonk stood hunched and menacing with an incredibly pained expression on his face. As all the eyes in the room rested on him, he looked much like he did when Terrabella had first seen him, fists clenching and unclenching, shaking with anger and ready to throw everyone into Ghastly Castle's dungeon. But this time, he also looked a little nervous.

Finally, he opened his mouth to speak. . . .

"I have to go to the bathroom!" squeaked Lord Thonk.

Then, with a cross-legged run, he raced away, never to be seen again.

And so, for years to come, it would be told that Lord Thonk was defeated by courage, daring and his own tiny bladder.

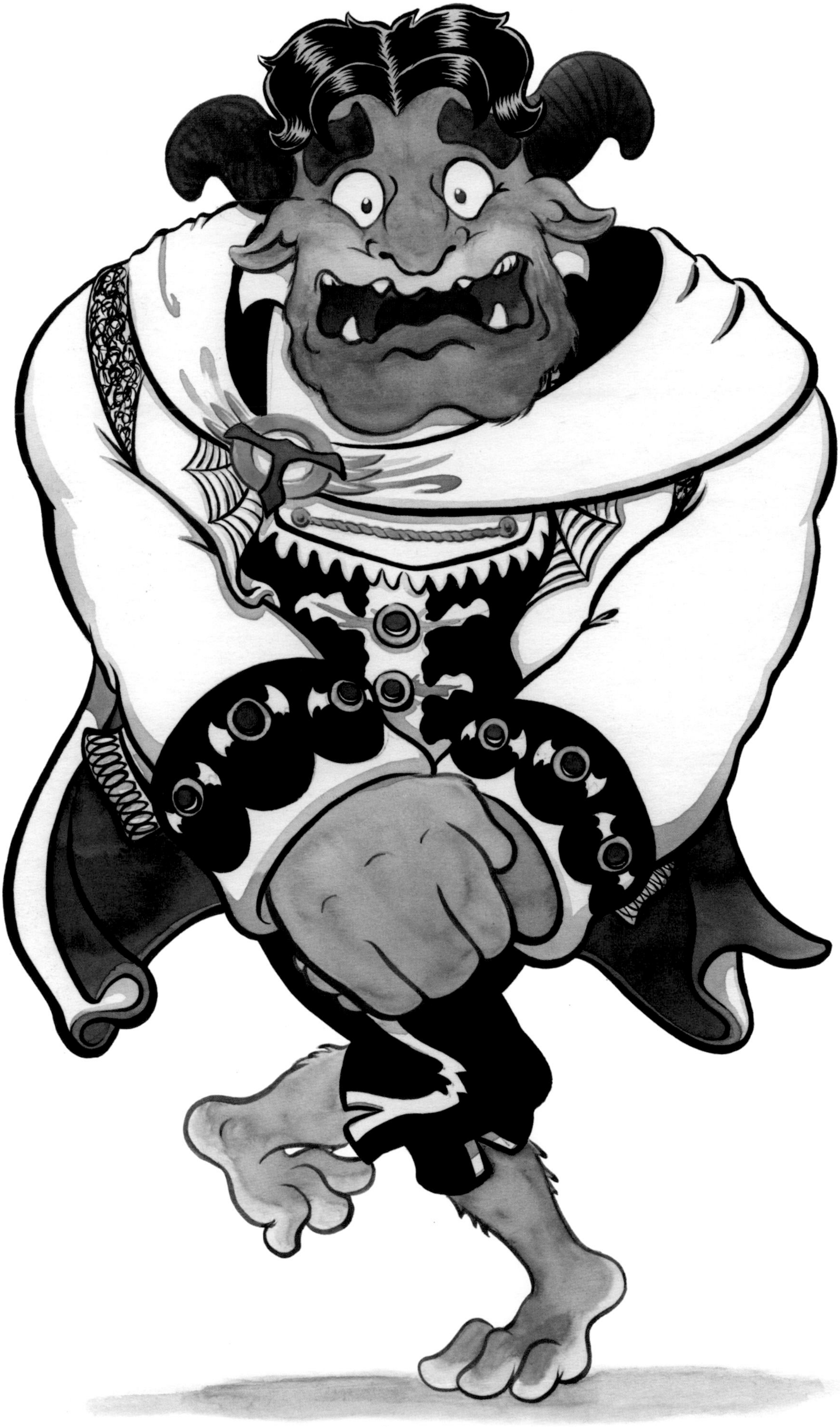

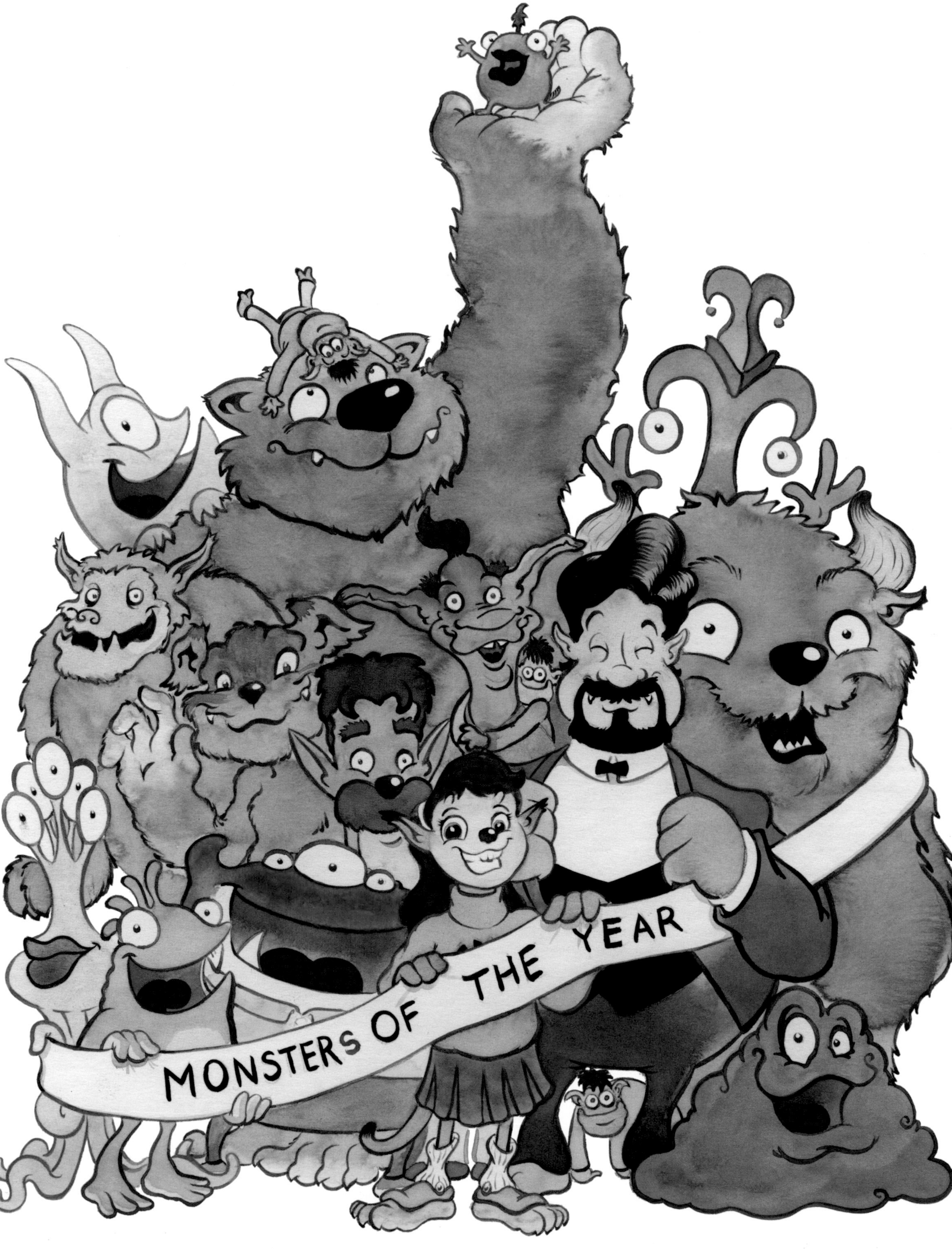
MONSTERS OF THE YEAR

After Lord Thonk's defeat it was quickly decided that the unsung monsters, and Terrabella of course, should all be made the Monsters-of-the-Year.

The celebration went on long into the night . . .

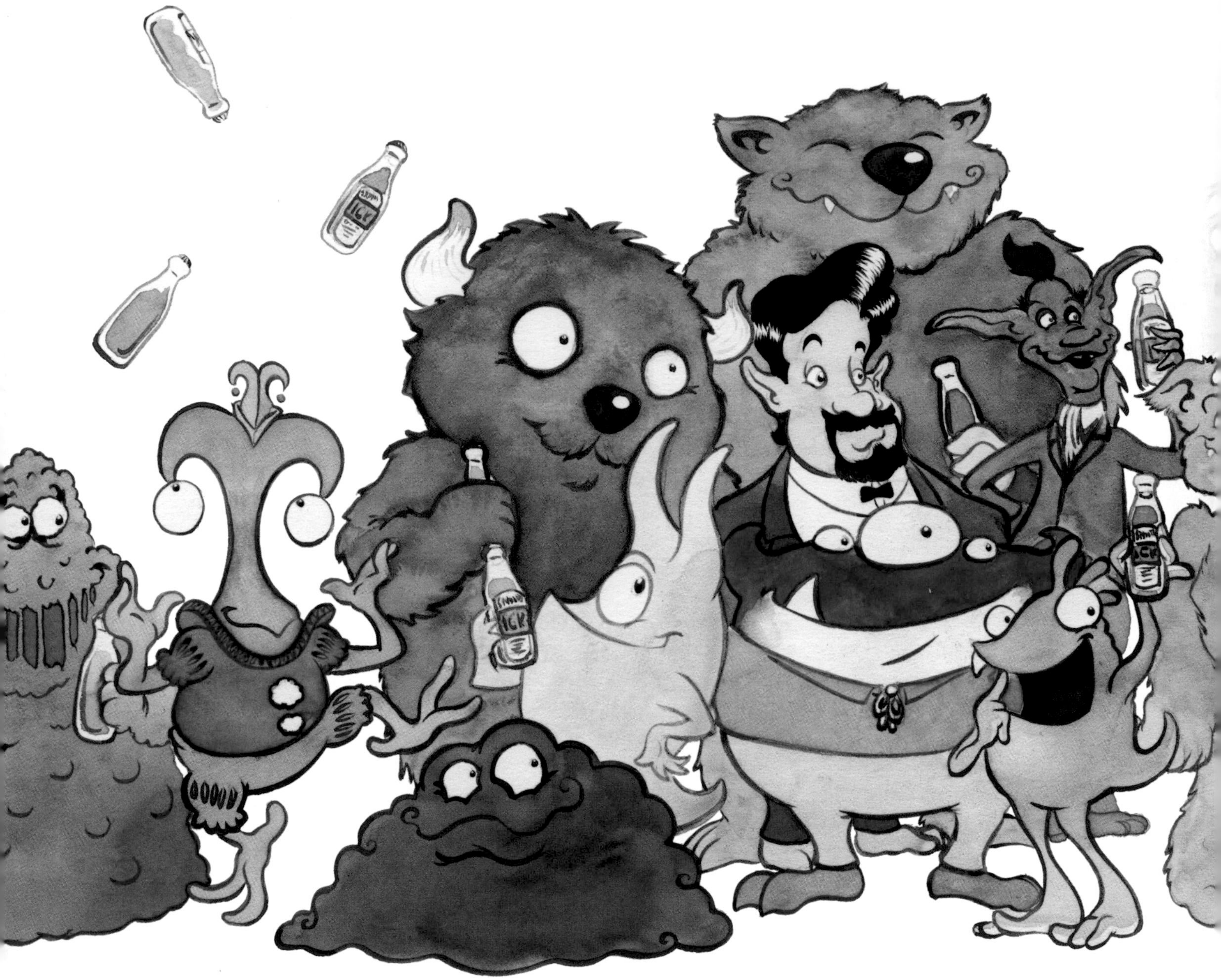
ICK
ICK
ICK

. . and everyone enjoyed Smoot's Ick.

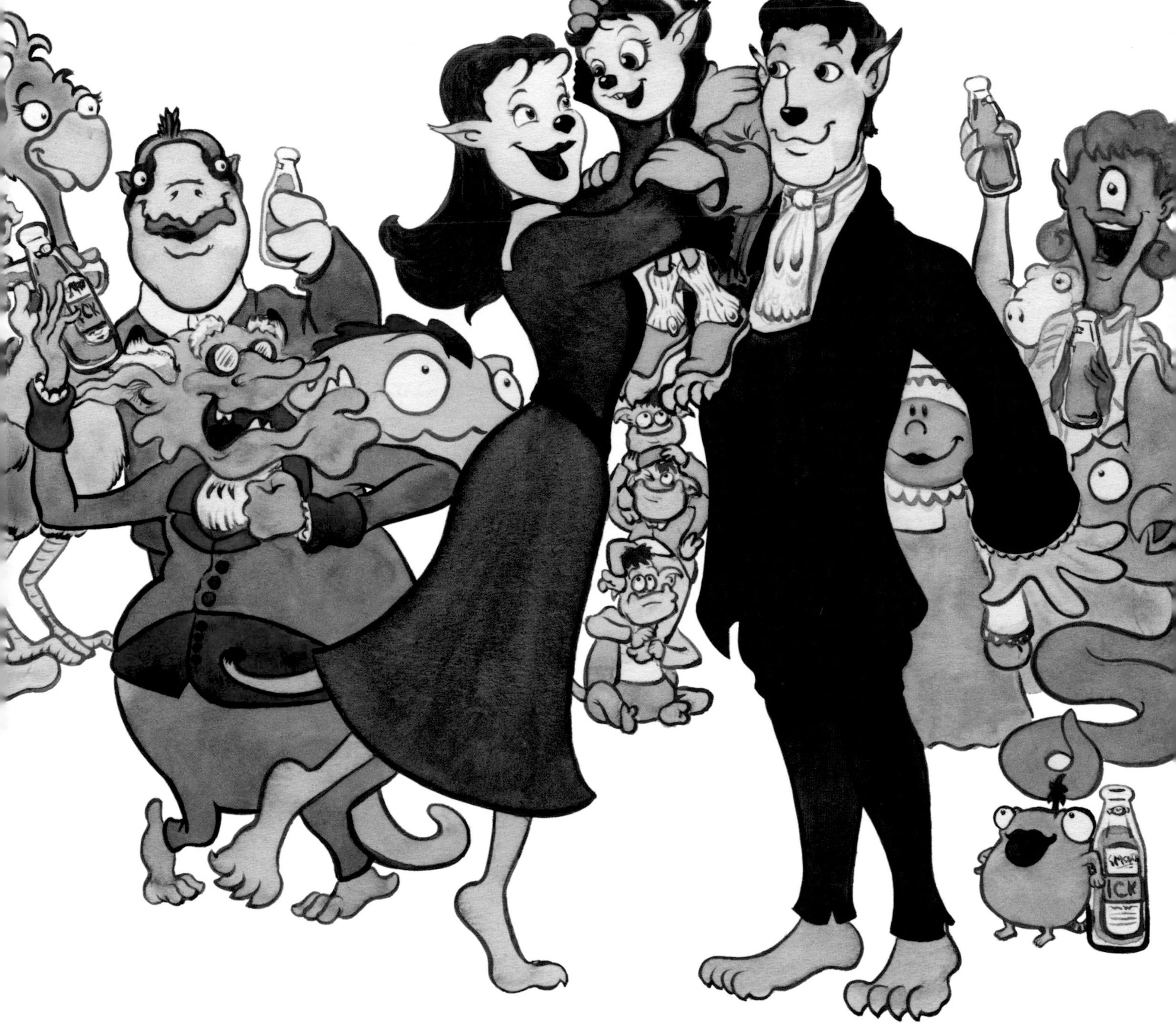
ICK
ICK

the end

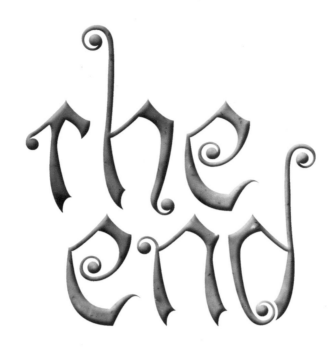

This book is dedicated to Terry, who watches monster movies with me.

Jon Hastings has had the nickname "Bean" since he was a kid and skinny as a string bean. He lives with his lovely wife Terry and their cats near Santa Cruz, California. He is the creator of the comic books "Smith Brown Jones: Alien Accountant," "Mad Science" and "Spark Generators." He likes comics, pirates, movies, books and pretending to be a monster by using roasted cashews as fangs.

You can find him on your computer at www.KiwiBean.com or write to him at KiwiStudios@Charter.net.

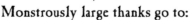

Monstrously large thanks go to:
Dan Vado and the fine folks at SLG; Bryan, Deb, Eleanor and Joe.
Jennifer de Guzman, Terry Hastings and Dawn Mortensen for helping to make my words sound real good.
My friends and family for their constant support of a crazed monster scribbler.

The illustrations in this book were done in watercolor on Crescent illustration board.
The font is Caslon Antique, Eppie's nifty words are in Poor Richard.

Terrabella Smoot and the Unsung Monsters, July 2005. Published by AmazeInk, a division of SLG Publishing, P.O. Box 26427, San Jose, CA 95159-6427.

For a free SLG Publishing catalog, call 1-800-866-8929. Visit us on the web at www.slavelabor.com. Printed in China.

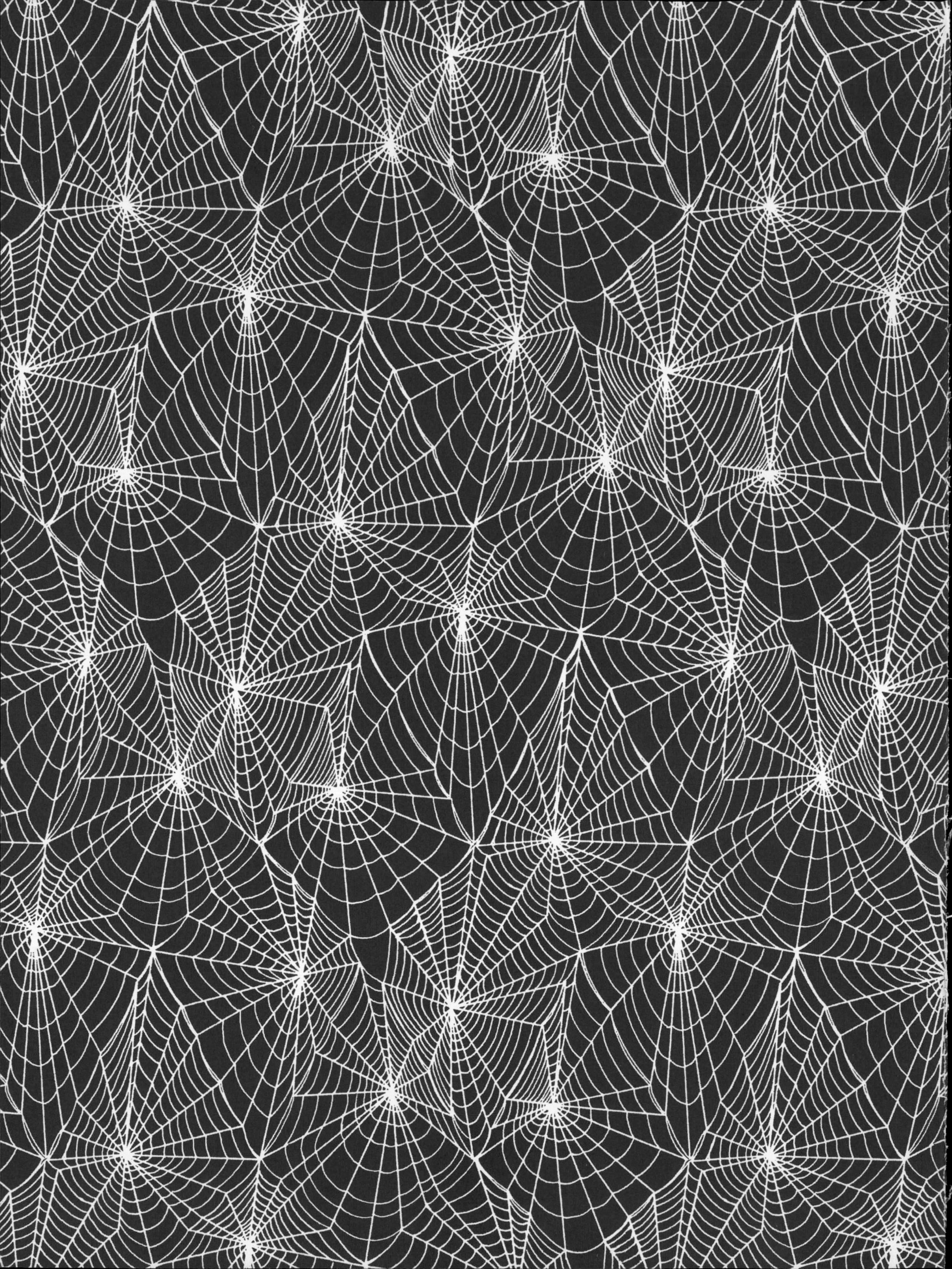